JN084484

Inbound/Outbound
Japan

Michael Pronko

Hisashi Tamai / Masaru Yasuda / Naoya Tashiro / Shiho Hashimoto / Tomoko Hashino

Kinseido Publishing Co., Ltd.

3-21 Kanda Jimbo-cho, Chiyoda-ku,
Tokyo 101-0051, Japan

First published 2020 by Kinseido Publishing Co., Ltd.

Cover design　　parastyle inc.
Illustrations　　Junichi Kishi
Photos　　　　　p.8 ©Marco Mancini; p.19 ©Ponsulak-Dreamstime.com; p.41
　　　　　　　　©Richard Gunion-Dreamstime.com; p.55 ©Andreas Altenburger-
　　　　　　　　Dreamstime.com; p.71 ©Marco Mancini; p.102 ©Marco Mancini

音声ファイル無料ダウンロード

http://www.kinsei-do.co.jp/download/4102

この教科書で DL 00 の表示がある箇所の音声は、上記 URL または QR コードにて無料でダウンロードできます。自習用音声としてご活用ください。

▶ PC からのダウンロードをお勧めします。スマートフォンなどでダウンロードされる場合は、**ダウンロード前に「解凍アプリ」をインストール**してください。
▶ URL は、**検索ボックスではなくアドレスバー(URL 表示覧)**に入力してください。
▶ お使いのネットワーク環境によっては、ダウンロードできない場合があります。

🔘 CD 00　左記の表示がある箇所の音声は、教室用 CD (Class Audio CD) に収録されています。

Introduction

Living in Japan for many years, I feel that I see more and more meanings and contradictions in Japan, and what I see makes me want to write. In my years in Japan teaching, writing, agonizing through the earthquake, and witnessing the economic downturn, political protests, attitude shifts and odd westernizations, I always feel like writing about my experience.

In some ways, Japan is built from words, so using words, organized into essays, can help to make sense of my experience of Japan. My experience might be the starting point for these essays, but each essay is an attempt to understand much more than my own experience. "Essay" in French originally meant "to try," and that is what I want to do in these essays, try to make sense of what I see and what happens to me.

The famous writer Henry James said that there was only one rule for writing well: "Only connect." That is, writing is a kind of connecting. I agree with that. As a writer and a teacher, I know connecting is the basis of learning and education. Ideas connect to people. People connect one idea to another idea. People connect to people, and the cycle of connecting grows. Connecting is essential for education, and essential for life.

For me, Japan has never completely normalized. There is always a little disconnection. I realize now that though I am very much in Japan, I will never quite be of Japan. I live here, but I am from another place. But that is a good position to write from—and in Japan maybe the only position to write from. The search for how and where I fit in—where I connect—and how I often do not fit in, gives me topics to think and write about.

These days, Japan is put into visuals—photographs, videos, anime, TV programs and films. I think that just looking at Japan is not enough. It is important to use words to help understand. Even visiting or living here is not enough. We have to think in words to really understand. Sometimes, video stops us from seeing, while words can make us see much better.

As the Zen Buddhists say, the finger pointing at the moon is not the moon. The essay pointing at Japan is not Japan. But then again, a finger or two pointed towards Japan can make everyone see more, think more and experience the world more deeply. That means taking joy in the differences, the similarities and everything in between. That means finding the deeper meanings.

E.M. Forster said, "How do I know what I think until I see what I say?" But for me in Japan, I always wonder: How do I know what I see until I read what I wrote about what I saw?

As an American who has made Japan home, I am used to confusion, of course, but then again, maybe "home" is a confusing word no matter where you live, no matter what culture, country or experience of life envelops you.

Of course, this is a textbook, and you will learn authentic English, but it is the process of reacting to the world and trying to explain my personal reactions that I hope you will learn from, too. That is an active process of learning how to see and learning how to express what you see.

As you read and think, you will start to get a sense of how you, too, can be both inbound and outbound. Inbound means paying attention, observing, reacting and feeling. Outbound means getting the courage to do something with English. Both of those are active processes and they are modeled in this textbook with the aim of you students doing something similar, in your own unique way.

Enjoy the journey in both directions!

Michael Pronko

Contents

PART I
Inbound Japan

Japan through an American Teacher and Writer's Prism

What's in a Name?

🎧 DL 002 ~ 014 ◉ CD1-02 ~ ◉ CD1-14

Walking back to the station after a party with my senior seminar students one evening, one of them suddenly turned to me with a serious look on her face and asked, "Can I ask you a personal question?" "Of course," I said. "What should I call you ex-
5 actly?" My first answer was going to be, "Call me Michael." Americans love to be called by their first names. The great American novel, *Moby Dick* by Herman Melville, starts out with the famous line, "Call me Ishmael." In America, a first name is part of your self-definition, a peg to hang your identity on. In Japan, though, it
10 is just not that simple.

All teachers are called *sensei*, a term of respect that establishes a clear social relation in a distinct hierarchy with clear expectations and obligations. As a *sensei*, I have duties to dispense, knowledge to pass on, and advice to hand out: in short, a well-defined role. Moving from *"sensei"* to "Michael" moves from the social to the personal, from the role to the person, a distance that in Japan is wider than in America.

Outside of school, what I am called does not always correspond to the precise formal terms of address Japanese use. The Japanese system of names and titles devolves into a puzzling jumble of inconsistencies with foreign names. On any given day, I might be addressed by any of the following: Michael, Pronko, Pronko *san*, Pronko *sensei*, Michael *san*, or Michael *sensei*. Each one indicates different degrees of intimacy and levels of social position, different levels of confusion. I have adjusted to living in Japan much better than my name has.

Japanese would always have *san* attached to their family name like *Suzuki san*. But the different foreign name order and often-unclear status means I have to be ready to answer to anything. At some restaurants I frequent, the master calls me "Michael *san*," but at others "Pronko *san*." However, sometimes it is the polite, formal master who uses the more informal "Michael *san*."

Anyone from the *takkyubin* home deliveryman to the department store service counter to the city office workers might call me "Michael *san*," too, just because "Michael" is in the front, left spot where Japanese family names usually go. I can never tell if the person is confused about my family name, or trying to act westernized, or just feeling close.

On the other hand, the young chef at a small French bistro I sometimes eat at, who always gives me a casual French hug when I leave, uses the more formal "Pronko *san*." I guess the casual hug and formal address go together in a mismatched Japanese way.

Some colleagues at university call me, "Pronko *sensei*"; others, "Michael *sensei*"; others, "Michael," but with no connection

to our relative age, closeness or protocol. One colleague I often go for a drink with still calls me, "Pronko *sensei*." Only now, as our friendship has deepened, it sounds ironic and joking. Switching now would involve an awkward negotiation. It is easier to leave it
5 as it is.

When speaking English, colleagues will sometimes refer to other colleagues by their first name, which makes me wonder: are they actually close or just using first names to fit the English culture usage? To switch from family name to given name means
10 switching an entire system of naming from one culture to the next, or to suddenly move several layers of intimacy closer. As with so many things in Japan, it is impossible to know.

My name almost never fits easily into application forms, forcing me to adapt and bend my name. At one point, I had three
15 different point cards for Yodobashi Camera, each with a different variation of my name. I'd forget the card and get a new one. A clerk would not let me combine the points, assuming I was three different people at the same address until I sat down with a manager and explained.

20 It was my fault for filling in the application form a different way each time, writing my name in the American order once, the Japanese order (family name first) once, and in *katakana* instead of *romaji* once. I tried to include my middle name, too, which does not fit in anywhere. "Which name is correct?" the manager de-
25 manded, but it was hard to say exactly. In Japan, I seem to have a rotating collection of names.

This tangled system of names will only get more perplexing as Japan internationalizes. One of my students who worked for a joint venture firm called her British boss, "Martin" but her Jap-
30 anese boss, "Sato *shacho*." The name systems cannot merge, but

12

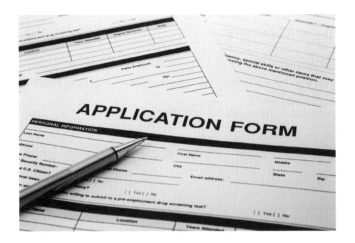

they can coexist.

Japanese like to stay inside their work titles, and reserve their first name for spouses, close friends or lovers. To become close enough to use someone's first name in Japanese is a powerful, moving moment. In English, your given name is used so often, 5 it could never carry such intense intimacy.

Nowadays, I use my first name more and more, with students, colleagues and even when I make a reservation at a restaurant. It is not closeness I want, but rather a bit of consistency. In Japan, anyway, no one is going to correct what you call yourself, 10 so like in some online avatar game, you can call yourself whatever you want.

I Using the keywords

In the blanks, put the most suitable word from the essay. More than one word might work, but choose the one that best fits.

1. If you can understand the social _____, you can see what position everyone is in compared to everyone else.
2. The names and the titles do not match exactly. There are just too many _____.
3. Those two friends have known each other for many years, developing _____ to talk about everything with trust.
4. To get the scholarship, I had to fill in many, many _____ forms, with every piece of information about myself.
5. In order to make a peaceful and functional society, many different kinds of people have to learn to _____.

II Comprehending the essay

Review the essay and find the answers to these questions.

1. What kind of problems did the writer find with his foreign name in Japan?

   _____

2. What is the difference between names in the west and names in Japan?

   _____

3. What kind of naming problem does he have at his university?

   _____

4. What kind of problems does he have with application forms?

   _____

5. What different meanings does a first name have in Japan compared to the west?

   _____

6. What does the writer wonder will happen as Japan interna-

tionalizes?

_____

Ⅲ Summarizing the essay

By reusing your answers to the comprehension questions, write a short summary of the essay in your own words.

_____

_____

_____

_____

_____

_____

_____

_____

_____

_____

Ⅳ Discussing ideas and opinions

Think about your opinion on each of these questions and discuss with other students in groups.

1. What names or ways of calling people show intimacy and close relationships?
2. Should Japanese names be written in western style or in traditional style in the future?
3. Which is better, using first names more or keeping exact titles with family names?

Unit 02

Country of Eyes

🎧 DL 015 ~ 025　　◎ CD1-15 ~ ◎ CD1-25

　　The other day, for the first time, a young woman on the train won the contest of "who will look away first." In the past, I could always stare longer than anyone in Japan, but this Japanese woman outstared me. I felt surprised, and a little humiliated, that

5　she could hold the eye contact longer than me—a westerner!

　　When I first came to Japan, shopping, teaching or just walking around, I felt bewildered because no one met my eyes. I felt alienated, anonymous, and unseen. Of course, I knew that in Asian countries, eye contact, like other body language, carries

10　vastly different meanings than in America. It shows respect and humility. Still, when eyelids would clamp down, I felt like the human element of the country was hidden away from me. It was hard to get a clear look into the heart of the country since the path through people's eyes kept getting blocked.

These days, though, Japanese eyes seem as comfortable with western as with eastern eye contact rules. Whenever I make a purchase or look around on the train, people do not look away like they used to. Their eyes linger on mine as they hand me my bag, sit across from me on the train, or cut in front of me up the escala- 5 tor. Has Japan changed, or have I? Or both? Japanese, especially in Tokyo, have always been masters of the side-glance and the stolen glance. But these days, Japanese are starting to master the direct stare, too.

I suppose some of this change comes from more Japanese go- 10 ing abroad. I can almost always tell when Japanese have spent a lot of time overseas from their eyes. In the same way that foreign words have crept into the Japanese language, foreign eye contact has crept in, too. Some people's eyes holler out, "Hey, how ya doin'?" To determine time spent abroad, eye-contact duration is as 15 accurate as any English language test!

Some people might interpret this is a loss of politeness. But it signals a big change in attitude. Keeping one's eyes cast downward used to express social position and respect, so the current directness may seem lacking in delicacy and courtesy. When I order 20 a coffee at the foreign-owned chain stores invading the country, I am startled by the way some young part-time workers look right into my eyes. It makes me think, "Where am I? New York?"

Yet, though it might sound strange, I feel somehow like Japanese eyes have been freed! They can look wherever they like for 25 however long they want.

Unfortunately, though, some Japanese probably feel they can look more directly because they are safe inside the technological insulation of their cellphone and earphones. For some of them, I guess, I am just another passing image. Looking at me is about 30

the same as looking into the eyes of a close-up of Johnny Depp (although I am maybe not as handsome) on their video screen. They may be looking more directly, and for longer, but not any more deeply. For some of those people, eyes are just an image of eyes,
5 nothing more.

Usually, though, for most people making eye contact, I think it is much more than that. Increasing eye contact shows people are not retreating deeper inside themselves, but coming out a little more. Japanese cities are, after all, relatively safe, with people
10 around all the time. For me, this increased eye contact shows an increasing comfort with other people, without any loss of civility. My students used to stare down at their desks so hard I thought there was something wrong with me, but these days, they are not afraid of confirming what they are hearing, or what they want to
15 say, through eye contact. They often look up, and a circuit is connected.

Even though we never say a word, the eyes I meet are filled with curiosity and warmth. They want to know what I am doing there, I imagine, and let their eyes linger a bit to find out. In Jap-
20 anese culture, it is always easy to look away, so I love these brief moments of ocular intimacy as I wander through the thousands of passing people every day. The increased eye contact shows people are unafraid to meet the inner world of some stranger in the middle of the city, even if for only a moment.

25 There is a lot to see in most Japanese cities, but despite all the attractions, the brief, little moments of eye contact offer beauty and intensity. So, different than observing another building, reading another menu or perusing another purchase, Japanese eyes express unfathomable meanings. What could be more beauti-
30 ful and mysterious than human eyes? What could be more human?

And every city in Japan has a lot of eyes to look into!

There is often a moment in the rush of life when I catch someone's eyes and feel stirred by some sympathy and connection that I cannot quite name. That moment, when eyes touch eyes, brief as it is, always recharges my human batteries. It reminds 5 me that Japan's huge and indifferent cities are really made up of people whose most interesting achievement is what their eyes, in their own special silent language, have to say.

In the blanks, put the most suitable word from the essay. More than one word might work, but choose the one that best fits.

1. When no one knows who I am in a large crowd, I feel rather
   _____.

2. Whenever I say goodbye to friends at the train station, we always _____ for a while and talk a bit more before we go our separate ways.

3. When I said hello to a stranger on the train, she gave me a strange _____ and walked away.

4. I tried to answer her question with a lot of _____ to not embarrass everyone, but it was hard not to be blunt.

5. She told me the truth, _____ my suspicion that something was wrong. I knew something was not right.

II Comprehending the essay

Review the essay and find the answers to these questions.

1. What happened to the writer on the train?

   _____

2. What did the writer notice when he first came to Japan?

   _____

3. How does the writer say eye contact in Japan has changed?

   _____

4. Why does the writer say eye contact 'rules' changed at first?

   _____

5. What other reasons are there for eye contact to change?

   _____

6. Why does the writer like to make eye contact?

   _____

III Summarizing the essay

By reusing your answers to the comprehension questions, write a short summary of the essay in your own words.

_____

_____

_____

_____

_____

_____

_____

_____

IV Discussing ideas and opinions

Think about your opinion on each of these questions and discuss with other students in groups.

1. Is eye contact a positive experience for you? Or does eye contact make you uncomfortable?
2. How does your eye contact change in different situations, at your part-time job, at home, with friends, at school? Why does it change?
3. How is eye contact a way of communicating? What messages can eye contact send?

Unit 03

The Language Dance

🎧 DL 026 ~ 038　◎ CD1-26 ~ ◎ CD1-38

　　As a foreigner in Japan, finding a language to converse in can be as confusing as interpreting the dance of a honeybee. In which linguistic direction should we fly? As an obvious English-speaking-looking person, I am constantly placed in the position of deciding what language to engage in.

　　I always start to talk with people in Japanese, but some of them, it occasionally turns out, speak better English than I speak Japanese. Before I can find that out, though, we have to perform the ritual language dance.

　　The ritual goes like this: I comment in Japanese about the weather; then, a few questions are asked about where I am from and why I am here; gradually, the other person will insert a word or two in English to kind of test the waters; and finally, if I catch the hint and ask a question in English—Presto! We switch around and enter an English conversation!

Or, non-presto, they nod politely and we remain in Japanese. It can take several polite rounds before we settle on one or the other, depending on our relative language levels, relative pride, or relative fatigue. At times, it feels like a pleasant decision, like 5 choosing either chocolate or vanilla, or both, but at other times, it feels like two sumo wrestlers grappling for the strongest hold.

This ritual is much more sophisticated than years ago, when English conversations mainly involved red-faced *salarymen* stammering drunk about my skill with chopsticks in a smoky bar. In 10 those days, too, random strangers on trains and high school kids on school trips to Kyoto, would try out their *eikaiwa* lessons on me, following the textbook patterns precisely. They treated me like a practice session.

Recently, though, people interact more naturally in both lan- 15 guages. They seem less afraid of conversations with foreigners— double strangers. The new-style English conversations are a sign Japanese English is getting better, and their cultural fearlessness is gaining hold.

Part of the problem is that my presence always provokes a 20 conversation about English, even when no English gets spoken. Slipping into a chair at the counter of a craft beer bar at the start of the summer, the voices of a middle-aged couple next to me lowered as I ordered a pint. They stole furtive glances at me. Then, I heard them whisper to each other *sotto voce* that was not so *sotto*, 25 "*Eigo zenzen dekinai!*"

But I am sure the woman at the counter next to me who denied being able to speak English could in fact order a beer in New York City if she had to. She felt provoked, obligated maybe, to discuss *my* language, as if I could not understand *hers*. But she did 30

not want to lean over for the ritual dance. Fair enough. But in her mind, I could tell, she was doing the language dance on her own.

At the start of the dance, it is always hard to gauge if someone really cannot speak English, in which case my forcing them into English would embarrass them, or if they are just being humble, in which case they actually want to speak English but hesitate in case I want to speak Japanese. They also want to be polite and not embarrass me, too, in case my Japanese is not up to it. So, we have to dance around a bit figuring out which language will best manage what we both want without imposing too much on the other. All of that happens in a few conversational turns, so I try to pay attention where the dance is headed.

I like it best when English helps us break out of the formal patterns and polite language, and lets the conversation fall into fresh exchanges. Japanese can really loosen up in English. After switching not just language, but cultural mindsets, people will often tell me more in English about themselves and their life than they ever would in Japanese. What emerges is something like: "I lived in Africa when I was young," or, "I worked in a restaurant in

London for ten years." I get more than just a conversation. English is central to the direction of their life, so the language reveals more than just their vocabulary score. It gives me their life story.

On the train from time to time, I like to peek over at lone uniformed students prepping for an English exam, moving their 5 red plastic sheet off and on their study list. Sometimes, the bedraggled student will look up, startled to see a real, live English speaker right beside them, as if magically conjured from the pages of the book.

I often give them my teacher's glare that says, "Study hard." 10 And if they are standing close enough, I like to whisper a friendly "*Ganbatte!*" The student, usually a girl, will blush as red as the plastic sheet that hides the answers below, and mumble, "Yes, I will, thank you," even if the words do not come out as anything more than a polite, silent bow. 15

For that student, still unsure how to pull the words off the page and let them live, the language dance is just beginning. I know that after a few more years of study, she will be engaging in the language dance, too, whichever direction in life her language study leads her. 20

In the blanks, put the most suitable word from the essay. More than one word might work, but choose the one that best fits.

1. I often find myself _____ in conversations that are very interesting.

2. Her wedding was very traditional, with many _____ like signing their names together and drinking *sake* at a Shinto shrine.

3. Probably you are suffering from _____ from overwork. You need a good rest.

4. He is very shy, and always has a hard time to _____ with people he does not know very well.

5. That _____ is very out-of-date. You should start thinking more like people do these days.

II Comprehending the essay

Review the essay and find the answers to these questions.

1. What happens when the writer tries to talk with Japanese people?

   _____

2. How is this "ritual" different than many years ago?

   _____

3. What does the writer think his presence causes other people to think or talk about?

   _____

4. What is the "language dance" exactly?

   _____

5. What is different when the writer speaks English with Japanese?

   _____

6. What does the writer wonder about when he sees a student studying on the train?

_____

III Summarizing the essay

By reusing your answers to the comprehension questions, write a short summary of the essay in your own words.

_____

_____

_____

_____

_____

_____

_____

_____

_____

_____

IV Discussing ideas and opinions

Think about your opinion on each of these questions and discuss with other students in groups.

1. Do you ever speak in English to new people? How do you decide which language to speak?

2. Have you been abroad? If so, did you converse in English? Did you meet anyone who could speak Japanese?

3. What are the main reasons most Japanese hesitate to speak in English?

27

Unit 04

Japan Open and Closed

🎧 DL 039 ~ 052   ⊙ CD1-39 ~ ⊙ CD1-52

Living in Japan is easier than ever before. It is not just that I can now find cheese and wine easily: even more amazingly, Japanese now love to eat cheese, too, and in fact are a bit picky about what kind of cheese they like. Even hanami parties have as much
5 wine as *sake*!

Japan has become more westernized, but that is not what I think is the best change over the last couple decades. Westernization has a good and bad side. When I say it is easier for me to live in Japan now than 20 years ago, I mean Japan has become more
10 open.

Japan now offers everyone, cheese-lovers or not, more choices about how to live and work and relax than in the past. In Japan, the range of lifestyle choices and the ways of thinking accompanying them, have expanded greatly, so that people can live more freely. Japan is not just a place; it is also an idea, one that keeps unfolding, and it keeps unfolding into more choice, more mental space, and more receptivity.

Of course, there are still plenty of rules. More than other world countries, Japan has maintained traditional social rules and customs. In many ways, Japan has changed more slowly than other big countries, saddled by a huge reserve of traditional ideas and unquestioned practices.

For foreigners, surviving in Japan requires learning the onslaught of such rules and practices. The more complex the interaction, the more complex the rules become. In Japan, social rules determine the way of shopping in a store, ordering in a restaurant, standing on a train or asking directions. For foreigners, the tremendous number of expectations can be exasperating and demanding. You can break those rules, and Japanese will not say much, but the rules are there.

To me, though, the constraints of Japanese culture always seem to be in a standoff with the openness of Japan's progressive trends. Japan is as much an idea as a location, and it is an idea often divided against itself. The free and open side of Japan stares down the conformist side like two sumo wrestlers in a long *shikiri*, poised for the initial charge at each other.

In past years, if I stepped into a small, out-of-the-way *izakaya*, I would often be greeted with wide-eyed panic by the staff and a hunkering looking-away by the customers. Would I speak Japanese? Would I like Japanese food? Could I follow the *izakaya* rules? Would I demand wine and cheese?

Nowadays, though, stores and restaurants are vastly more receptive and less concerned about an unusual person stepping into their midst. If anything, I miss being noticed all the time.

Nowadays, people worry not about my foreignness messing up the smooth Japanese flow of things, but whether I will appreciate the beauty of their place. They want to explain how special the appetizer is or how high-tech some new eyeglasses are. I am no longer
5 disrupting the harmony. Japan's harmony now encompasses diversity.

Conversations in Japan used to be rather dull. I was asked constantly about whether I could adapt to Japanese life. It used to be a big mystery to most people here why I would choose to live
10 in Japan since I was not born here, transferred here, or married here. That used to be confusing, since they could not understand how any non-Japanese would end up living in Japan.

Now, though, Japanese understand the appeal of Japan as a place to live, work, love and play. The pleasure and wonder of
15 living in Japan seems obvious to most Japanese I talk with. Japanese have a sense of pride born of a newly appreciative view of their country. The idea of Japan has expanded and loosened, and as that has happened, it has become a place not just to end up, but more importantly to choose to be in.

In a conversation with a taxi driver about the need to get ready for the Olympics as we pulled into Shinagawa station, I complained about the disorganized taxi line outside the station. "Ah, now you're thinking like a Japanese," the driver said. I took that as a compliment, one that would have been impossible in 5 years past, when the driver would have said something defensive like, "Well, there's a lot of people and cars in Tokyo," as if I had not noticed. But that driver and I both had the same complaint!

I often still sense the cold wind of strict rules or traditional obligations that limit how freely foreigners—and Japanese—can 10 live. But when I feel the iron grip of those constraints, I know that I can always shift my attention towards the more open sides of Japan, to the music clubs, the small movie theaters, the odd fads, the unexpected conversations, and the many different ways of thinking, working, living and enjoying oneself. 15

The sheer range of human choices pushes the country's life into greater openness. Though sometimes slightly hidden, the freedom and openness of Japan is always ready and waiting.

By which I mean, I can always find really good cheese.

I Using the keywords

In the blanks, put the most suitable word from the essay. More than one word might work, but choose the one that best fits.

1. She is very _____ about what she eats. Only certain foods are OK for her, and not very many kinds.
2. I had to fill in the application form ten times. It was so _____ to have to do it again and again until it was correct.
3. High school uniforms always seem very _____ to me. Everyone looks the same.
4. She is not very _____ to criticism. In fact, she hates it.
5. I never listen when someone gives me a _____. They are just being nice to get something in return, I feel.

II Comprehending the essay

Review the essay and find the answers to these questions.

1. What does the writer say about Japan westernizing?

   _____

2. What does the writer say about the many rules in Japanese society?

   _____

3. Has Japan become more receptive in the writer's opinion?

   _____

4. What does the writer mean when he says, "Japan's harmony now encompasses diversity"?

   _____

5. What does the writer say about Japanese pride in Japan?

   _____

Ⅲ Summarizing the essay

By reusing your answers to the comprehension questions, write a short summary of the essay in your own words.

_____

_____

_____

_____

_____

_____

_____

_____

_____

Ⅳ Discussing ideas and opinions

Think about your opinion on each of these questions and discuss with other students in groups.

1. Do you think Japan is becoming more open than before? That is, are there more choices for young people than for past generations?

2. Is Japan an easy country for foreigners to live in, in your opinion?

3. Japan, like most Asian countries, is often described as a closed society. Do you agree with that idea? Why or why not?

Unit

05 Why Ask Me?

🎧 DL 053 ~ 065   ⊙ CD1-53 ~ ⊙ CD1-65

I was sitting at a ramen counter for lunch when an older, perhaps retired, man next to me asked, "You like ramen?" "Of course,
don't you?" He chuckled, "I'm Japanese, so of course, I like ramen!"
"Well, I love ramen, too," I assured him. He asked me a few more
5 ramen specialty questions about oiliness, flavors and other ingre-
dients, and appeared amused by my detailed knowledge. Then, we
got back to slurping, but I thought, why ask me?

This same interrogation happens all the time. Do I like *sake*,
sushi, *natto*, chopsticks, bathing at night? I get a whole list of
10 questions. Whatever I say, people are impressed. But I am always
surprised that Japanese think only Japanese can truly enjoy Japanese culture.

Of course, the super-naïve questions I got years ago are no
longer as common as they once were, with "Can you use chop-

sticks?" being the classic. Japanese have moved the cultural dividing line further inside as they have more contact with foreigners. But still, I have to assure people, no, no, I truly feel *sashimi* washed down with a glass of *sake* is a bit of heaven and I am genuinely awed by the old-wood beauty of Japanese temples. I really 5 am. I am not just pretending.

I do draw a line at *shiokara*. Some Japanese hate it but I wonder are the *shiokara*-hating Japanese somehow less Japanese? Does the "*shiokara* line" divide cultures or individuals? I probably eat more ramen than most Japanese but does that mean I *am* 10 more Japanese than they are? Did that retired ramen-lover experience ramen from inside his culture, while I was enjoying it from outside, at a distance? Were we united as noodle-lovers, or experiencing entirely different bowls?

In New York, no one would ask a foreign visitor if they enjoy 15 eating a juicy steak. No Parisian would ask a non-French person if they enjoy drinking a glass of wine. It is a given. It is obvious. It is a pure pleasure, not some expression of being American or French.

But in Japan, certain experiences are claimed as Japanese. But are Japanese pleasures just for Japanese only? I wonder if 20 Japanese who attend an *ukiyoe* woodblock print exhibit are doing some sort of cultural homework assignment, or do they personally feel the prints are beautiful and interesting? Are Japanese savoring a rock garden in Kyoto expressing their inner Japanese character or searching for individual enlightenment? It seems to 25 me that staring up at the serene face of the Buddha in the spacious hall of an ancient Japanese temple would strike wonder into anyone's heart, regardless of what culture they come from or what religious beliefs they have.

Being Japanese seems to include an automatic copyright to 30

a big catalogue of cultural activities. You do not have to actually suffer repeated kicks and throws in an *aikido dojo* or apprentice yourself for years to a master pottery craftsman, as a couple of my non-Japanese friends have done. Japanese think you just have to be born Japanese and all that Japanese culture belongs to you. Japanese often claim the rights to their cultural triumphs, even without doing anything themselves.

The reluctance to share those rights and let experiences transcend cultural boundaries is centered in justifiable pride. Transcending does not come easy to many Japanese. When boundaries are opened up to let anyone in, culture moves from ritual activity to broader considerations. Who owns the experience of a certain taste? How is appreciation learned or acquired? Which comes first, individual likes or cultural imperative?

Asking is a way of re-claiming heritage, and by asking at least Japanese break their usual wall of silence to interact with a stranger. But that moment of seeing me do something Japanese is also, I guess, a bit threatening. So, that question is also a way of re-asserting cultural difference, and, at other times, I like to imagine, it is a way of opening up.

I wonder what other parts of Japanese culture will become accepted around the world. *Sushi* and animation films have become globally popular partly because of their exotic Japanese uniqueness, but also because they tap into universal desires—for 5 meaningful fantastic stories (*anime*) or unprocessed freshness (*sushi*). People from many, diverse cultures can share the pleasure of a story and of a taste, and in many cases, appreciate it the same, and sometimes even more.

Japanese culture will get a massive reconsideration as more 10 and more people around the world turn their attention to Japan. Maybe we will find out what parts of Japanese culture are more broadly lovable, as more people start trying out everything from *yakitori* to cat cafes to *geta* to *shiokara*, though I doubt the latter two will catch on worldwide. 15

I wonder if Japanese will keep asking non-Japanese why they like Japanese things, or if they will come to accept that Japanese culture shares a great deal with other world cultures. As more tourists come to Japan, more and more of the hidden-away sides of Japanese culture will come out into the light, to more uni- 20 versal acclaim and acceptance, and maybe understanding, too.

As for ramen, how much more universally lovable a lunch could there be?

I Using the keywords

In the blanks, put the most suitable word from the essay. More than one word might work, but choose the one that best fits.

1. I get tired of endless _____ about where I am from.
2. She has so much _____ to answer, because she is shy.
3. There is always a _____ between cultures, but that can be _____ by understanding.
4. With enough patience and study, you can develop an _____ of cultural differences which are hard to understand at first.
5. Are cultural values _____, or are they individual choices?

II Comprehending the essay

Review the essay and find the answers to these questions.

1. Why did the man ask the writer about ramen?

   _____

2. What do Japanese think when they see the writer enjoying Japanese things?

   _____

3. What does the writer say about *sashimi, sake* and old temples?

   _____

4. Does the writer say the same things happen in New York or Paris?

   _____

5. In what ways do Japanese take pride in their culture?

   _____

6. What does the writer wonder will happen as more tourists come to Japan?

III Summarizing the essay

By reusing your answers to the comprehension questions, write a short summary of the essay in your own words.

_____

_____

_____

_____

_____

_____

_____

_____

_____

_____

IV Discussing ideas and opinions

Think about your opinion on each of these questions and discuss with other students in groups.

1. Why are Japanese surprised when non-Japanese like something very Japanese?
2. Who owns cultural values and activities? Only the culture of origin, or can anyone claim it?
3. Will Japan become more like other cultures or will Japan keep its specialness in the future?

Politics So Far from Home

🎧 DL 066 ~ 076   💿 CD1-66 ~ 💿 CD1-76

One question I always get as a foreigner in Japan is: What do you miss about home? Of course, I miss big-cut French fries, classic rock radio and driving on wide streets. But I also miss the insanity of American politics.

5　　Reading about the latest scandal, election, speech or debate, I feel the pull of America. It reminds me of the mixed-up good and bad of America's politics: its brashness, posturing, and outspoken-ness. From my perch in Japan, I feel like I am watching an alien culture in some distant galaxy. Strangely, I miss it.

10　　And yet, the media in this day and age bring politics almost as close as if I were actually living in the States. Whether I am in Tokyo or in Chicago, I can watch the latest gaffe and absurd pro-nouncement from any politician in America, or in the world. What really brings it close is not the media, but the irritation I feel!

I miss arguing about politics. Get into any American taxi around election time and you have a political discussion whether you like it or not. I especially miss one of America's most overt political expressions—the bumper sticker. The hilarious slogans, sarcastic comments and political joking on the back bumper of 5 cars lets you react: either "What a moron!" or "True that!"

Bumper stickers are the place where Americans express themselves openly to anyone driving behind them. In Japan, there are campaign trucks, but on a daily basis, few people openly proclaim their politics. Japan probably has the fewest bumper 10 stickers of any country in the world, though hanging candidate's posters on walls is similar. Japanese posters, though, tend to have earnest slogans and serious poses. American bumper stickers are meant to provoke an argument, or make an ironic comment, even if, as it usually happens, you never see the car again. 15

I also miss knowing right away what people's politics are. In Japan, I find it hard to guess who people vote for: does the cute OL on the train vote LDP? Or do the retired people going to a flower exhibit vote Communist? My students squirm and frown when I ask them directly, as do most of my colleagues. In America, though, I can always tell someone's politics, because politics is worn on the outside, always ready to ignite, especially during campaign season.

5   Politics is important because it is where passions reside. When I watch the election primaries and early speeches of candidates, I feel that Americans relish the conflict of politics and take pride in disagreeing openly. "Let's agree to disagree," is a phrase everyone in America learns as a way to respect others' opinions, or
10 at least stop an argument. Or sometimes, it is also a way to argue in a softer but continued way. But in Japan, respect for others' opinions is more often expressed through unspoken means.

Sometimes people assume you give up the right to opinions about domestic politics when you live abroad. They assume if you
15 live someplace else, you do not care. But I think it is just the opposite. I might vote by absentee ballot but I still shout at the screen when I see some small-minded, out-of-touch comment by one of the candidates. My life might be in Japan now, but my outrage still lives in America. The longer I live here, the more irritated I
20 get at Japanese politics, too, but that is still a later, learned irritation. It is not my default mode.

I suppose it is remarkable I feel so aggravated when I watch the Republicans or Democrats campaigning on the other side of the world. And I am always surprised when their misguided com-
25 ments and unwise proposals can still enrage me when they are so far away. But they do. From time to time, I feel irritated about Japanese politics because the problems seem so similar: the betrayal of trust and chronic bad decisions. But here, it is a less instinctive reaction. You only get angry at what you care about.

30   I cannot say I like feeling angry every time I hear a candi-

date spout foolish opinions, but it feels natural to be upset. Maybe, until I quit feeling so angry with them, and start feeling just as angry about Japan's politics, I will never quite be transformed into a real Japanese. Politics is as much a home as where your house is. What you feel is where you live. 5

And then, there is relief when the emotions can finally turn into a vote. I cannot wait to get my hands on my absentee ballot. I often find myself writing to my representatives, even if they are in another country. I feel the need to express myself no matter how far away I get. And you can probably guess who I vote for, even if 10 you do not read my bumper stickers! In Japan, I have to put my bumper stickers on my refrigerator. But they are there prominently!

I Using the keywords

In the blanks, put the most suitable word from the essay. More than one word might work, but choose the one that best fits.

1. Politics for him is nothing but an _____. He does not like to read, talk or think about it.

2. I always know when the _____ is coming in Japan. Trucks drive through the streets announcing the candidates.

3. I do not even know all the _____. There are so many people running for office, it is hard to know them all.

4. It is _____ that so few people vote. You would think that many more people would want to express their right to vote.

5. When a politician does not do what they promise, it feels like a _____. It feels like you have been cheated unfairly.

II Comprehending the essay

Review the essay and find the answers to these questions.

1. Why does the writer feel a pull from America?

   _____

2. What kind of political things does the writer miss?

   _____

3. What is the writer's feeling about bumper stickers?

   _____

4. What does the writer find confusing about Japanese politics?

   _____

5. How are politics and passion connected in the writer's opinion?

   _____

6. Is politics passionate in the writer's opinion?

   _____

III Summarizing the essay

By reusing your answers to the comprehension questions, write a short summary of the essay in your own words.

_____

_____

_____

_____

_____

_____

_____

_____

IV Discussing ideas and opinions

Think about your opinion on each of these questions and discuss with other students in groups.

1. Do you pay close attention to politics? Why or why not?
2. Do you agree that politics is less open and more private in Japan? Why is it more private in Japan, do you think?
3. What bothers you most about politicians and politics in Japan?

Unit 07 Is Japan in Decline?

🎧 DL 077 ~ 087　🔘 CD1-77 ~ 🔘 CD1-87

　　According to many recent articles, Japan is in decline. The articles paint a disheartening picture of Japan. Most of the articles focus on Japan's stalled economy, the stagnant political system and the weight of providing for a graying population. Education is
5　portrayed as out of touch with the changing world. The picture in those articles is grim indeed, but is Japan really in decline? The question is a tough one.

　　Most of the recent articles come from economic analysts. They look for business growth, usually in the short term. When
10　looked at from that point of view, Japan's economy does not inspire optimism. Debt is growing and the economic data show little growth. However, those reports tend to examine profit-oriented criteria. They are not wrong, but they do not take a broader view, and maybe western ways of analyzing simply do not fit Japan.

Most of those economics-based articles compare Japan to its "bubble era," when the economy was booming. The current picture looks worse than then, of course. But it also looks worse partially because Japan was perhaps overpraised at that time. Books and articles then were amazed at the successes of Japan. They took many of Japan's business practices as perfect models for the West to copy. Japan seemed to be an Asian miracle. But was it? Or was it just a country working hard to improve itself? And what would that mean—"Asian miracle"? Isn't every country a miracle in its own way?

The Japan-loving books generated a reaction from "Japan-bashers." These Japan-bashing writers criticized Japan for being too socialistic, or too controlling, and noted the suffering of workers forced to do overtime and bosses given too much power. They pointed out the short-sightedness of the enduringly low position of women in Japanese society and the exam-obsessed educational system. Which view was correct? Was Japan an economically efficient business paradise or a grinding place of overtime and exhaustion and unfairness?

Surely, both lovers and bashers were right to some degree, but not entirely. Both sides — Japan-lovers and Japan-bashers — took too extreme a view, as do many articles now. Japan's economy is still the third largest economy in the world, or fourth largest if the European Union is considered a single economy. That is not bad for a shrinking, graying population living on an island in the Pacific Ocean. In fact, it is not bad for anyplace at all.

The argument can be made that Japan is relying on borrowed money, but that money is being spent. Everywhere one looks in Japan new projects are taking place. New train lines are being built, skyscrapers scrape the sky more than ever before, and night-time

areas are packed with people enjoying themselves. Japan's big cities seem to be redoing themselves to make more room, and more convenience, for everyone. Part of the dynamism of Japan is not in the economic figures, but in the ways that budgets are being
5 spent.

Of course, the argument for sluggishness is easy to agree with. Growth seems slow and uncertain. However, Japan has an energy to it that visitors admire and Japanese admit. Wherever one looks in Japan, everything from government offices to the po-
10 lice to retail companies are still functioning. The way they function can surely be criticized, as too slow or too old-fashioned, but every day, progress is made.

What is needed is a more realistic view of Japan, about the strengths and weaknesses of the country overall. Japan is unlike-
15 ly to overtake China, but that does not mean it is in decline. The European Union and the United States both have big problems in their economies, too, but few articles declare them in decline. Perhaps that is because economic analysts tend to come from the west.

Without a doubt, the problems facing Japan are tough ones. The problems of joblessness, suicide, nuclear power and the position of women in society deserve greater attention and action. Japan has few inspiring political leaders. Education needs an overhaul and oppressive workplaces need to be reformed. Without 5 addressing these problems, Japan might tip to the decline side. But if those problems can be corrected, it will not decline.

For every problem, you can find a positive to balance it out. Japan has a strong sense of social cohesion and an ongoing respect for skilled work and quality products. The group mentality can be 10 too much at times, slowing individuality, but social connections run deeper than in many countries. The basic trust in democracy has not been corrupted. Japan's cultural life is energetic, with urban living, food, film, literature and creative expression of all kinds still vibrant. The convenience and safety of everyday life is 15 an enduring part of society. Few other countries have as extensive or as efficient a system of public transportation as Japan has. That system connects all sides of life, and keeps them going.

With a more realistic view of itself, one that takes the negative and positive sides in equal measures, Japan can begin the 20 hard work of moving forward again. Shared goals create a sense of forward motion and progress, and those goals are not destroyed by self-interest as often happens in other countries. The problems of the past still linger, and need correction, but the idea of decline in Japan seems to encourage harder work more than a feeling of 25 giving up. With that spirit, Japan can reshape and rethink itself in positive and meaningful ways.

In the blanks, put the most suitable word from the essay. More than one word might work, but choose the one that best fits.

1. That kind of bad news is so _____. It makes me want to give up.
2. I have _____ that this project will work out just fine. In fact, I am sure of it.
3. If we divide up this task and each does one part, it will be more _____. We can do it better and quicker without getting tired.
4. Big cities always have a great deal of _____. The energy level is very high and it seems like so much is happening.
5. She is a very _____ person, always talking and socializing very enthusiastically.

II Comprehending the essay

Review the essay and find the answers to these questions.

1. What view of Japan is found in many recent articles?

   _____

2. Why do the economists compare Japan to the bubble era?

   _____

3. Which side, Japan-lovers or Japan-bashers, is more correct, according to the writer?

   _____

4. What signs of dynamism does the writer point out?

   _____

5. What problems does the writer point out?

   _____

6. What does the writer mean about having a realistic view of Japan?

III Summarizing the essay

By reusing your answers to the comprehension questions, write a short summary of the essay in your own words.

_____

_____

_____

_____

_____

_____

_____

_____

_____

IV Discussing ideas and opinions

Think about your opinion on each of these questions and discuss with other students in groups.

1. Do you feel Japan is in a boom or a slump? What examples do you have for your opinion?
2. What are the biggest problems that Japan faces in the near future?
3. What strengths does Japan have that will help it to progress?

Unit 08

A New Era or An Era of Newness?

🎧 DL 088 ~ 099   ⊙ CD1-88 ~ ⊙ CD1-99

I was as surprised as everyone when the name for Japan's next era was announced. It was not so much the name itself, Reiwa, as how it was chosen. Basically, no one knows how it was selected. It seemed like maybe it was decided by cabinet mem-
5 bers, bureaucratic committees, scholars of Japanese classic litera-ture, professors specializing in imperial history, and the Imperial Household Agency.

I wondered who were these people? Why was everything so secret? Why *should* it be kept secret? Maybe I got off on the wrong
10 foot with the new era, but all the secrecy rankled me.

And then it became more secret. Papers and magazines re-ported some of what was happening, but most took place far from the public eye. There were all kinds of secret rituals at restricted shrines and sacred grounds. I imagined an entire undisclosed world of mysterious activities involving swords, mirrors, *torii*, chrysanthemum images, rice stalks, *sake*, and intensely colored silk costumes. Shouldn't that *all* be on TV?

Even though I felt disappointed not to see more of those rituals, the era change was a big event. Like the rituals, I think the 5 biggest changes, though, were unseen. Those changes took place inside people. It was as if Japan had a new mental and spiritual OS installed. Maybe that is what all those secret rituals were about?

Like most people in Japan, I suppose I started wondering 10 what the future will hold. A new name should mean something new. I am sure that the emperor and his family will act in distinctive ways, but what really impressed me was how the hope for Japan's rejuvenation and revitalization floated in the air.

The change is certain to be interesting. My students feel 15 something has been handed down to them. It is not easy to describe what they felt they were given, but I think it was a sense of taking up challenges. Japanese young people are often criticized for being passive and introverted, and that is certainly true. I could write several essays on *that* topic, but the real meaning of 20 the era change will depend not on the name or rituals, but on how young people interpret it, and what they do about it.

Many young people act as if history and society hang like weights around their ambitions, holding them back. The era change might be a chance for them to participate more, or at least 25 feel they can, and to start escaping from the traditional hierarchy where they feel stifled. In the next era, maybe, their hard work, skill sets and ambitions will not have to wait in line before they can show what they can do.

That is particularly true for women, who still find themselves 30

underrepresented in positions of power and have a hard time getting around the traditional mindset that constrains them. My only regret about the new era name is that it did not include any reference to women. But maybe the discussion was started already
5 over whether the next emperor could be an empress. The new era will be about women, no matter what happens, because they are still the most underdeveloped resource in the country. Resources, at least, do not stay hidden for long. The vibrancy and energy I see in my women students must go somewhere: into politics, work, so-
10 ciety and fresh attitudes.

As a teacher, of course, I also hope that the new era will find ways to change outdated educational practices. A recent survey of OECD countries found Japan ranking lowest in several categories: classroom activities with no fixed answer, activities demanding
15 critical thinking, and activities involving IT and communication. That result was a bit startling because those are *exactly* the kinds of skills needed in the future workplace.

And speaking of workplaces, Japanese junior high and high school teachers are the most overworked in the entire world. Ed-
20 ucation should be given top priority, not just by the government, but by parents, students, teachers, businesspeople and everyone connected to learning, which is, in fact, everyone! Give teachers a chance to restore their humanity and to study and learn more, and they will be better at helping others to do the same.

25 It is not just teachers that are overworked, though, almost everyone is. Japanese are reluctant to use even their allotted vacation time. Ironically, the week of the era change was one of the first times in decades where workers could take a long vacation. If that is the start to the new era—more time off—I am for it! Va-
30 cation is not just fun, it is integral to the efficient and productive

functioning of any job. The first lesson long-distance runners learn is how much rest and recovery time they need.

Even if they are secret, I think the ancient imperial rituals of Japan should be maintained. They offer a beautiful spectacle and rich symbolism, and maintain important bonds with the past. But 5 at the same time, I hope the era change will spur a deeper look at what works in Japan and what does not, to see the country more honestly and directly, in order to start moving forward towards what works better. The new era has the initiative and momen- tum to transform the country in positive directions. If the new era 10 name and the old rituals help do that, they will have performed their most vital function.

I Using the keywords

In the blanks, put the most suitable word from the essay. More than one word might work, but choose the one that best fits.

1. Access to this area is _____. You must have permission to enter.
2. What is most _____ about Japan are the many unique rituals that are different from most other countries.
3. He seems to have no _____ whatsoever. He does not want to achieve anything or even be promoted.
4. That way of thinking is extremely _____. No one thinks like that these days.
5. The change in her appearance was _____. She was surprisingly different.

II Comprehending the essay

Review the essay and find the answers to these questions.

1. What did the writer wonder about the new era name of Reiwa?

   _____

2. Why did the writer start thinking about the future of the new era?

   _____

3. What does the writer say about young people's attitudes?

   _____

4. What does the writer say about women in Japan?

   _____

5. What does the writer suggest about the future of education?

   _____

6. Does the writer want to get rid of the old secret rituals?

   _____

Ⅲ Summarizing the essay

By reusing your answers to the comprehension questions, write a short summary of the essay in your own words.

_____

_____

_____

_____

_____

_____

_____

_____

_____

Ⅳ Discussing ideas and opinions

Think about your opinion on each of these questions and discuss with other students in groups.

1. Do you agree that many young people are passive and introverted? How can they change in the new era?
2. Do you think the future will be good for women in Japan? Or will it be the same as in the past?
3. What is the importance of not overworking and taking vacations in your opinion?

Earthquake Life

🎧 DL 100 ~ 112 ⊙ CD2-02 ~ ⊙ CD2-14

Earthquakes, small or large, make me feel like an animal about to be pounced on by a predator: I look around, adrenaline pumping, ready to run, panicked to get away from the violent earth. Often as they come, earthquakes are a part of life in Japan
5 to which I have failed to adapt.

Before I came to Japan, I knew there were earthquakes here, but I did not worry about it much. My first earthquake arrived as I was writing a letter in my first sublet apartment. The building was so cheap and old I thought at first it was the wind rattling the
10 windows and shaking the cupboard. (I am from Kansas, home of tornados.) But as my coffee spilled over the half-finished letter, I realized what it was. It made a great letter home.

Earthquakes change you. Their unpredictability sinks into your consciousness, or unconsciousness, and changes how you think about life. More earthquakes came along and each one added anxiety. The unpredictability of earthquakes frightens me, but it also reminds me of what it means to be human—never knowing what the future might bring.

When a quake hits, the real conversation is internal—between body and mind. Earthquakes run only an intense few seconds. But they seem much, much longer, since everything instantly doubles in concentration and confusion. The body says go. The mind says stay. Both speak loudly. I wait, thinking what earthquakes always make me think, which is, "Is it getting worse, or slowing down, or is this the big one?" There is no way to out-plan, out-think, out-prepare them. Earthquakes are an immense force you can do little about.

How Japanese really comfort themselves about the prospect of an earthquake remains a mystery to me. I asked my Japanese friends what they do and think, but when it comes to earthquakes, they clam up. They shrug their shoulders and coolly reply, "What can you do?" or "We Japanese are used to it!"

I like that stoic attitude, but it seems at times to be the old "*shoganai*" attitude. I have learned that Japanese approach to ignoring things like smashed toes on the train, or a shockingly high bar bill. It works pretty well. But the ability to ignore earthquakes is something I still cannot master. It seems a baffling mix of passive acceptance, pragmatic realism and transcendence. Learning about earthquakes after the age of 30 is like learning to drive a car or swim at that age. You kind of get it, but it never feels natural.

When the big earthquake hit in 2011, I was at home. I ran outside and stood in my garden. The next-door neighbors ran outside, too. The wife fell to the ground holding her teenage daughter's hand and clutching their dog. As we tried to stay upright on the trampoline of the earth, I said something to calm them. That comforted me, but it was still the most terrifying few moments of my life.

5   The odd time after the earthquake transformed even a big city like Tokyo from exciting and dynamic to silent and calm— like during the New Year. Little by little, I started to feel everyone might be helpful to each other. People became polite and unobtrusive, and much more attentive and focused, more aware of each other and their environment. A newly aware mindset sprang from respect for the fatalities, concern for the survivors and self-reflection about the past and future. If a strong one hits, everyone will have to work with strangers, take care of them or be taken care of by them. In Japan, everyone became a little less of a stranger.

15   For months after the disaster, I felt discombobulated, a word I had always read, though never used. The word fit this odd, new reality. The old routines no longer worked. Everything felt strange, as if we had all been let out of the hospital after a long stay. I went through the motions of all my usual activities, working, shopping, going out, but none of them felt the same. The disasters broke up and washed away the old feeling of normal.

To comfort myself during that recovery period, I stuck to routines like taking care of my garden. A couple months after the big quake, I went to buy plants and soil at the home center. The clerk who helped me took my payment and then looked at me, reached across the counter and shook my hand. He thanked me for staying in Japan and not fleeing after the quake.

So many foreigners left after the quake, newspaper columns and online blogs branded them *"fly-jin,"* a rhyme with *"gai-jin,"* the deprecating word for foreigner. They were edgy with fears of radiation from the damaged nuclear plant and the nerve-rattling aftershocks. Even my colleagues at university asked me if I was going to leave, while my friends and family kept offering their homes back in the States.

Surprised by the clerk's comment, I could only mutter, "I live 5 here." "I can see that," the clerk answered, smiling and wrapping my plants carefully.

As I biked away with my soil, vegetables, seeds and fertilizers, I almost went back to tell him I was not planting everything new as a selfish luxury, when so many had suffered, but as a way 10 to ease my sadness after seeing so much destroyed, and as a way to rekindle the hopeful energy that I always felt was the engine of Japanese life.

I Using the keywords

In the blanks, put the most suitable word from the essay. More than one word might work, but choose the one that best fits.

1. I was so terrified, my body's _____ kicked in and made my heart beat fast.
2. The _____ of earthquakes makes them scarier. You never know when they will happen.
3. She is very _____, always thinking about the most reasonable and realistic thing to do in a practical sense.
4. The number of _____ was so sad. That many people dying is just terrible.
5. Having a car feels like a _____. I do not really need it, and it is expensive, but I love driving on the weekends.

II Comprehending the essay

Review the essay and find the answers to these questions.

1. What happened during the writer's first earthquake?

   _____

2. What happens to the writer when an earthquake hits?

   _____

3. How do the writer's Japanese friends react to earthquakes?

   _____

4. What happened to the writer at first during the 2011 earth-quake?

   _____

5. How did the earthquake change things?

   _____

6. What happened when the writer went to buy things for his garden?

   _____

III Summarizing the essay

By reusing your answers to the comprehension questions, write a short summary of the essay in your own words.

_____

_____

_____

_____

_____

_____

_____

_____

_____

IV Discussing ideas and opinions

Think about your opinion on each of these questions and discuss with other students in groups.

1. What is the best thing to do when an earthquake hits?
2. Do you think Japan was permanently changed by the big 2011 earthquake?
3. Do earthquakes, or other tragedies, have a way of creating bonds among people? How does that happen?

Unit 10

Integrating Immigrants

DL 113 ~ 123   CD2-15 ~ CD2-25

When I first came to Japan, there were so few foreigners living here, people would stare at me, point and whisper. That never bothered me so much, since Japanese were alternately nice and shocked at my presence. People helped me, even if they were sur-
5　prised. To open my first bank account, I sat with the branch manager, a dictionary and two staff to complete the all-Japanese form. They could not have been nicer, even though I was probably the first foreigner ever to have a bank account there.

One day, the doorbell rang and I stepped out to see a delivery
10　man holding a big box. When he saw me, though, he fell backward off the porch step. "Ah, ah, ah, *gaijin!*" he said, dropping the package. I asked him if he was all right. I had never knocked someone over just with my face before.

That would never happen now. Foreigners are everywhere,

64

especially in big cities these days. But back then, there were so few non-Japanese, I would often strike up a conversation with complete strangers. I would speak to people from Africa, the Middle East, and Asia, all of us feeling a kind of bond. I could go for weeks without seeing another foreigner outside the English Department of my school. 5

I left Japan for six or seven years and when I returned, things had changed. There were more foreigners, most of them interested in discovering an authentic experience of Japan. The idea was to sink deep into Japanese culture and find its essence. Japanese were more stand-offish—not unkind, just distant. *"Nihongo o-jozu desu"* people would tell me constantly, regardless of whether I spoke correctly or not. Perhaps for them, a foreign person speaking any Japanese at all was worthy of comment. Westerners avoided each other and Asian immigrants tended to form their own, slightly insular communities. 15

After more tourists started to come to Japan around 2010, things changed again. Whereas before, I ignored foreigners, resident or not, I suddenly started to help lost foreigners. I live on the Chuo Line which passes through Mitaka, the closest station to the Ghibli Museum. Almost every commute for a few years, I rescued some group and rode with them back to Shinjuku. If there was a foreigner in a restaurant or shop, I sometimes helped translate. On the street, I pointed them the right way and often added a recommendation for a good ramen shop. I felt it was my duty. 25

Nowadays, though, there are too many tourists to rescue anyone. No one compliments my Japanese. I see foreigners almost every day. The response to me is changing. Recently, Japanese get a little impatient if I do not explain myself in clear Japanese. And there are areas of the city with more and more immigrants. It has 30 been a long time since I have had a class of only Japanese students without at least one student of mixed heritage or different nationality.

But all those changes are nothing compared to what is likely
5 to happen in the future. Immigration will continue to shape Japan, though I wonder how much. At times, I am amazed at Japan's resistance to change and the resilience of traditions. But I am equally amazed when things shift towards a more open attitude and an embrace of difference. It used to be, say, a French restau-
10 rant was the translation of French cuisine by a Japanese chef who studied in Paris, and the food was modified to fit Japanese taste. But nowadays, a French restaurant in Japan is just as likely to have an actual French person cooking authentic cuisine.

Immigration, as well as emigration, has made the boundaries
15 of Japan more fluid. As that has happened, I do not think Japanese customs, cohesiveness or culture have started to collapse. Just the opposite, immigration and emigration seem like a gentle wearing away of the inflexible sides of Japanese society to reveal what is strongest and most valuable inside. Japan has long had
20 *omotenashi*, but that attitude can only be seen in practice. The arrival of immigrants is not a loss of identity, but rather a clarifying of Japanese-ness.

Japan will have to get beyond simply *omotenashi* as more immigrants arrive. A deeper integration of immigrants is needed,
25 without such strict boundaries between inside and outside, Japanese or non-Japanese. That does not mean losing Japanese things; it means doubling them. Cultures in proximity will inevitably come into conflict, but there is a type of conflict that spurs constructive growth and, eventually, respectful harmony.

30 Japan has a strong, central culture that has persisted for

centuries, so there is no chance Japan will evolve as other multi-cultural, heterogeneous countries like America or Brazil did. Those countries were of mixed origin from the beginning. In contrast, Japan is adding immigrants to an already vibrant homogenous culture. The house is built, but the furnishings might change.   5

Will blips and glitches occur as more foreigners immigrate to Japan? That is almost certain. But the trick is to find how to work together. The challenge—and the hope—is to find an interactive, synergistic blend for different kinds of people where everyone gains, and no one loses. It is easy to dwell on the downside of im-   10
migration, but it is hard to work towards an attitude and system that enhances the benefits. If so, Japan just might become the first heterogeneous homogenous culture on earth.

I Using the keywords

In the blanks, put the most suitable word from the essay. More than one word might work, but choose the one that best fits.

1. This Thai food tastes good and very _____. The cook must be from Bangkok.

2. The _____ of his argument is easy to grasp, but the details are too complex to remember.

3. I am American but my family's _____ is Russian and Swedish, but that was several generations ago.

4. There is always _____ to change. Many people like to stay the same because it is easier and more comfortable.

5. The main difference between _____ and _____ cultures is the degree to which different kinds of people and of thinking are accepted.

II Comprehending the essay

Review the essay and find the answers to these questions.

1. What experiences did the writer have when he first came to Japan?

   _____

2. How did Japan change when the writer came back after several years away?

   _____

3. How did things change when more tourists starting coming?

   _____

4. What does the writer imagine will happen in the future?

   _____

5. What will maybe have to change as more immigrants arrive?

   _____

Ⅲ Summarizing the essay

By reusing your answers to the comprehension questions, write a short summary of the essay in your own words.

_____

_____

_____

_____

_____

_____

_____

_____

_____

Ⅳ Discussing ideas and opinions

Think about your opinion on each of these questions and discuss with other students in groups.

1. Have you ever helped a foreigner in Japan?
2. Is it a good thing to have more immigrants to Japan from different countries? Why or why not?
3. Will Japan change because of all the immigrants? Or will Japan become more Japanese?

PART II
Outbound Japan
Global Mindset for the Future

The Right Amount of Confidence

🎧 DL 124 ~ 135   ◉ CD2-26 ~ ◉ CD2-37

Japan has the least confident students in the entire world. Anytime and anyplace, students will tell you directly, "I can't speak well!" And they mean it! But it is not only students. I meet serious, suited 50-year-old businessmen who blush and shyly
5 wave their hands like schoolgirls who say the same: "My English is bad." Hipsters dressed all in black in a club will suddenly lose their cool, start escaping towards the bar, and say, "English? *Heta. Heta heta!*" As a foreigner, I hear this chorus of self-pity all the time!

10   This does not happen in other countries. Traveling around the world, people may be good or bad at English, but they never have the teeth-sucking panic that Japanese have. Why does this happen in Japan? The question is not an easy one, and surely the answer is different for all students of English. And since almost

everyone in Japan studies English at some point in their lives, almost everyone in Japan is an English student, current or former. How can the entire country be lacking confidence in English?

Of course, Japanese culture values humility. Bragging or being overconfident is totally inappropriate in the world of Japa- 5 nese politeness. The attitude of unassuming modesty is a pleasant thing, and is very different from America where young people often put on an act of cool self-possession that can be very grating. However, "High Anxiety" and "Low Confidence" seem to be the prerequisite courses for English study. 10

After teaching low-confidence students for years, I now make it clear to them that when learning a language, a certain degree of poise and self-assurance is absolutely necessary. Displaying confidence in English is not always arrogant or selfish, but simply part of communicating. The lack of confidence becomes an irritating 15 restraint to comfortably speaking another language. As with any endeavor in life, finding the right balance of confidence and humility is not easy, but it is at the very heart of using English well.

The consequences of not learning appropriate confidence can be disastrous. Most students get sidetracked into permanent anx- 20 iety that flusters them with even a basic English interaction. For many students, their English becomes arrested at a low level simply because they never learn how to act confident enough to even *start* practicing English. They lose energy in the struggle to find confidence, which then makes them avoid more practice, which in 25 turn keeps confidence low.

Does the school system create this vicious cycle of diffidence? It seems unable to break that vicious cycle. One way to start breaking that is to think of learning language as a dramatic activity that needs a "willing suspension of disbelief." I have to suspend 30

my real view of my students and treat them as better than they really are. When I do that, they begin to act at a higher level of confidence. The act eventually becomes reality, and they acquire confidence. This is not an easy process, and often ends up with a
5 degree of over-confidence, but that is still better than being stuck in childish fears and uncommunicative panic. It is one way out of the cycle.

Every so often in a small class, I ask students to grade their own papers. This always confuses students, because the teacher
10 is supposed to do the grading. I explain that I want them to see their English, and their writing more clearly. I want them to grade themselves honestly and think of the reasons why they give themselves the grade they do. When I do this, though, only a handful of students ever grade themselves appropriately; the vast majority
15 grade themselves much too low. No one ever grades too high.

Why is that? I always wonder. The answers are different for every student, but one thing that always emerges from forcing students into self-evaluation is that they are not able to see their own work very clearly. Their confidence comes from test scores or
20 objective evaluations, not from their own clear view of themselves.

Genuine humility always accompanies genuine confidence. What students need to learn is that speaking, writing or using English involves a certain degree of self-aware surety in order to proceed. Like acting on the stage, confusion, anxiety and a bumbling
25 approach create their own kind of disaster. Apologizing before or after speaking does not help communicate; it makes it harder.

As a teacher, one of the benefits of being 'on stage' every day is that the ability to appear confident becomes part of your life. I do not always *feel* confident inside, but outwardly, a display of
30 confidence sets the students in class, or an audience for a presen-

tation, at ease. They can relax, I can relax, and then the communication can take place.

Japanese cultural values cannot be changed, of course, but they do not need to be. Being confident, assertive, and self-aware are values demanded for success in modern life. Those values do 5 exist in Japanese culture. Many Japanese have strong confidence in their own abilities for many different areas of life, especially after a lot of practice. Strangely, English is not often one of those areas.

One should not be overconfident, but if students learned the 10 ability to express a confident attitude in English, they would gradually and naturally develop genuine confidence, not a false one based on test scores or false compliments. Of the truth of all this, I am very, very confident!

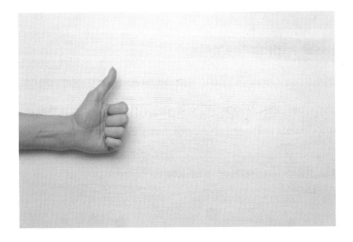

Using the keywords

In the blanks, put the most suitable word from the essay. More than one word might work, but choose the one that best fits.

1. Before a test, I am always in a _____. My anxiety level shoots up and I find it hard to concentrate.

2. She always accepts her awards with _____. She never thinks she is better than other people, and works hard for the next one.

3. When you give a speech, be sure to maintain your _____. Acting confident will help you communicate your ideas more easily.

4. It is hard to remain _____, but try to put aside your personal feelings and consider the facts in a neutral way.

5. She is very _____ about her own opinions, but she is never too strong and never forces anyone to agree with her.

Comprehending the essay

Review the essay and find the answers to these questions.

1. What does the writer think is different about Japanese and other countries' people about English?

   _____

2. What does the writer say about the importance of poise and self-assurance?

   _____

3. How can students break the vicious cycle of lacking confidence?

   _____

4. How do Japanese students grade their own papers?

   _____

5. Why is acting confident important?

6. Do Japanese cultural values need to be changed?

Ⅲ Summarizing the essay

By reusing your answers to the comprehension questions, write a short summary of the essay in your own words.

Ⅳ Discussing ideas and opinions

Think about your opinion on each of these questions and discuss with other students in groups.

1. Why do most Japanese lack confidence about speaking English, in your opinion?

2. What is the best way to develop confidence in using English, in your opinion?

3. What is your best technique for learning and using English?

Mistake Makers of the World, Unite

DL 136 ~ 146   CD2-38 ~ CD2-48

One of the false impressions created by drowning students in grammar exercises, fill-in-the-blank worksheets and multiple-choice tests is that language has right and wrong answers and that's it. The picture you get from neat, little blanks and a
5 100-point grading scale is that native speakers communicate in perfectly formed, correct, error-free sentences all the time. That's a laugh. Real language, especially spoken language, is loaded with mistakes.

In fact, everyone who speaks any language does so in sloppy,
10 stumbling, stuttering messes of linguistic mush. Much of what people say is gobbledygook. People hesitate, change words, get confused, cough, stop mid-sentence to think, and say things like, "Wait, wait … I mean …" then totally reverse the entire message they just delivered. That is just how people are—full of mistakes!

If humans can be said to have a single unifying characteristic, it would be their mistake-making capacity.

However, my students never want to make any kind of mistake. They erase half of what they write, imagining it is wrong. They stay quiet if they do not know the perfect way to explain 5 their opinion. They look through the dictionary for a long time for one single word. And sometimes, their fear of mistakes stops them from doing anything at all!

Students are worried about mistakes because they have been taught to be. Some teachers correct mistakes before the student 10 has even finished the sentence. They hand back writing covered in red corrections. They make students redo the form of their work, without even getting to the content of what they are saying or writing. This teaches students to be afraid of mistakes, but it does not teach them English. 15

Mistakes are not good, but are entirely normal. Not only do adults make mistakes in what they say all the time, but just listen to kids in their first language. They make a lot of "mistakes," especially when they go through their language growth spurt. Gradually, they find what is correct. During their language learning, 20 kids can drive you crazy asking questions, forming longer and longer sentences and rambling on all day long. But that is how you learn. I wish my classes were as noisy as a bunch of three-year olds!

Instead, what I often get is silent, stony-faced young adults 25 too afraid to speak in case they utter one single mistake. English classrooms, though, should be places to make a lot of mistakes, without worry, and not have them corrected too much. Most English classes in Japan are basically "mistake correcting" classes. My college students are shell-shocked survivors of chronic correc- 30

tion!

Children, teenagers and adults have brains at different stages of learning development, and so need different kinds and levels of input, but the similar point is a constant flow of language. Not
5 worrying about mistakes lets language flow more easily. Most mistakes students make can be corrected later. Mistakes will always happen. They are no big deal.

Mistake making cannot be changed, but the attitude towards mistakes can be. When learning a language, mistakes have a nat-
10 ural percentage, like missing free throws in basketball or pitches in baseball. No one thinks of missed free throws or strikes as mistakes. That is because even the best athletes can only hit, at the very best, 80 percent free throws, and an even lower percentage of baseball pitches. While learning or practicing sports, these per-
15 centages are even lower. Sportspeople just try to get the percentages up. Mistakes show you are in the game!

We often laugh at speaking mistakes in everyday life because we know nothing bad will happen. They are just "words, words, words," as Hamlet said when asked what he was reading. A good laugh at mistakes can change the atmosphere in the classroom. A mistake-ready classroom ensures that the fear of mistakes does not become ingrained and harmful. In mistake-ignoring and mistake-welcoming classrooms, learners feel comfortable to try to correct mistakes on their own, or just laugh at them, forget it and 5 move on. Connecting mistakes to laughter helps learning more than connecting mistakes to shame.

The attention on *what* is said is more interesting than on whether it is *correct* or not. If a student says to me, "You is a good teacher!" I would not stop and correct the verb, but rather I would 10 feel flattered and pleased. We can still communicate even with mistakes. Focusing on content rather than mistakes allows learning to flourish without fear, shame or self-correction. We should listen for content, not for mistakes.

Life is too short to pay attention to all the mistakes. Some- 15 times, I think the world is divided into two kinds of people: those who learn from their mistakes; and those who are embarrassed by them. We make too many mistakes anyway to pay attention to all of them, and the ones we do notice, we can learn from. We have to learn to love our mistakes, respect ourselves when we make them, 20 and let plenty of mistakes flow through our lives.

I **Using the keywords**

In the blanks, put the most suitable word from the essay. More than one word might work, but choose the one that best fits.

1. His handwriting is so _____ I cannot even read half of what he wrote.

2. Everyone has the _____ to learn, but that does not mean it is easy.

3. The fear of mistakes is deeply _____ but that fear can be overcome and a new attitude learned.

4. I was very _____ to receive the award. It was a wonderful recognition for my work.

5. Students almost always _____ in a supportive, clearly organized and encouraging environment.

II **Comprehending the essay**

Review the essay and find the answers to these questions.

1. According to the writer, how is language usually used?

   _____

2. What is the attitude of most students towards mistakes?

   _____

3. How are children learning their first language and most students different?

   _____

4. What is the writer's attitude towards mistakes?

   _____

5. What is the importance of focusing on content in communication?

   _____

Ⅲ Summarizing the essay

By reusing your answers to the comprehension questions, write a short summary of the essay in your own words.

_____

_____

_____

_____

_____

_____

_____

_____

_____

Ⅳ Discussing ideas and opinions

Think about your opinion on each of these questions and discuss with other students in groups.

1. What is your attitude towards making mistakes?
2. Why do some students worry so much about making mistakes?
3. Do you agree that sometimes mistakes are helpful? Why or why not?

Unit
13 The Art of Conversation

🎧 DL 147 ~ 157   ⊙ CD2-49 ~ ⊙ CD2-59

To truly learn a language does not mean learning just the rules and sentence parts, but getting a feeling for beauty and meaning. Language is a vast sea of cultural ideas, creative expressions, and complex meanings. To handle all these intricate and
5 powerful ideas, and to get to the beautiful, meaningful nature of language, what is most needed is art, not structure. Learning a language is really learning the art of conversation.

People who learn languages well are usually not so good at grammar; but they are always very good at conversation. They
10 know the art of conversation, a skill that involves basic human qualities: an interest in people, the ability to listen carefully and ask good questions, and a degree of personal warmth. That is the art.

This human art of conversation is not easy to teach. Grammar is much easier, since it is condensable into worksheets and right and wrong answers for tests. Grammar has a definite starting and stopping point, and can be handled with efficiency and order. Art, however, is subjective, messy and undefined. Art takes a long time to set up and get going, and is hard to stop just because 5 the bell rings for the next class. It does not fit school schedules easily.

Most speaking books give short conversations, so students get the idea that conversations are just a few lines long! Here is a typical textbook example: 10

Maria: Excuse me, can you tell me where the Smith Building is?

Ken: Sure, go down this street to the stoplight, then turn right and it's straight ahead.

Maria: Is it a big building?

Ken: Yes, quite big. You can't miss it. 15

Maria: Does it have "Smith" written on it?

Ken: I'm not sure. Listen, I'm going in that direction. I'll just show you.

This kind of practice conversation is about grammar practice. It is not very interesting. It does not sound real. 20

In contrast, real conversation can be endless. I have a Japanese friend who always asks me question after question when I talk with her. I forget I am even talking because she can create a flow of exchange that never seems to stop. She says things like:

That's interesting. I never knew that. 25

What do you mean by that?

Where did you learn about that?

Why do you think so?

I wonder why that is.

How did that happen? 30

She also tells her opinions and little stories, too, but the conversation with her always remains fascinating because she knows how to engage fully in the conversation. Her grammar level is only so-so, but her conversation level is exceptional. I wish English 5 textbooks taught those conversation-extending and conversation-deepening phrases.

Using conversation to learn a language would mean focusing on universal human values rather than memorizing rules or acquiring structures. Conversation is an art that rests on an abil- 10 ity to give and take, to be honest and clear, and to feel pleasure in the exchange of language. The best conversationalists express a delight in exchanging viewpoints, making jokes, hearing what another person really believes, and considering the world from another point of view. This understanding connects to the attitude 15 that conversations are good opportunities to learn something, feel something, and express something.

What makes a good conversationalist? Of course, knowing some grammar rules helps, but *only* knowing the rules helps you very little. Instead, conversation involves a few easily learned 20 techniques such as conversation starters, topic changing phrases, follow-up questions, or open style questions. A few idioms can help, and for English, the ability to interrupt helps a lot, too. Some non-verbal 'tricks' like looking more directly in people's eyes if they are from western countries, nodding one's head to signal "I 25 am listening," and responding quickly also help to keep conversations going.

Mostly, though, the art of conversation is built on real questions that come from natural curiosity. Some people are good at getting you to talk and keep talking. That is not a fake ability, but 30 a genuine interest in knowing more, learning more, hearing different and unusual ideas, and being unafraid to express one's own thoughts. That can be a bit scary at first, but is exciting as well. Conversational artists know how to get past the grammar rules to open people up, explore ideas, discover feelings and enjoy language. 5

Great artists, like great conversationalists, know how to keep talking in interesting ways because they know something more than just rules. Over-emphasizing grammar closes off discussion and communication. It stops conversation from happening because once the right answer or perfect sentence is found, everything 10 stops. Students get to the end of a few lines of textbook conversation and they do not know how to keep going. They answer a question, but then stop, and do not respond more.

What a different language classroom it would be if everyone were supposed to become great artists of conversation rather than 15 perfect test-takers. If schools thought of language more as an art of dynamic exchange than as a static set of rules, then students would find it much more beautiful, human and meaningful to speak English, and they would come to love the art of conversation. 20

I Using the keywords

In the blanks, put the most suitable word from the essay. More than one word might work, but choose the one that best fits.

1. That student always asks _____ questions that help to understand the most important points of the topic.

2. That movie had a very complicated plot, which is not _____ to just a few words.

3. His essay was truly _____. No other student ever wrote a paper quite as unique as that one.

4. Our class discussion was really fascinating because we could hear many different _____ from all the members of our group.

5. Most students are too shy to _____ the teacher during a lecture, but they often ask questions after class.

II Comprehending the essay

Review the essay and find the answers to these questions.

1. In addition to rules and sentence parts, what else is important for learning a language?

2. Why is conversation important when learning a language?

3. What does the writer suggest about being good at conversation?

4. How does conversation help learn a language?

5. What makes a great conversation artist?

6. How would language classrooms be different if they empha-

sized conversation instead of taking tests?

III Summarizing the essay

By reusing your answers to the comprehension questions, write a short summary of the essay in your own words.

IV Discussing ideas and opinions

Think about your opinion on each of these questions and discuss with other students in groups.

1. What is the most interesting conversation you have ever had? Why was it interesting?
2. Do you agree that conversation can be a helpful part of learning language? Why or why not?
3. Do you agree that emphasizing rules too much makes learning a language harder? Why or why not?

Unit
14 "Get Out! Why Not Go?"

🎧 DL 158 ~ 169   ⊙ CD2-60 ~ ⊙ CD2-71

In my classes, I often tell my students, "Get out!" I am not throwing them out of the classroom; I am encouraging them to get out of Japan to study abroad. Japanese university students are often hesitant to study abroad, but I argue that nothing could be
5 more important. Why not go? I ask them. You can always come back.

The education ministry has been doing more than asking questions. It is offering money! To encourage more students to study abroad, the ministry announced it will offer funds for uni-
10 versities to expand and improve study abroad programs. I hope that will happen, but I have my doubts. Japanese young people feel so comfortable in Japan—maybe too comfortable.

For many years, the number of Japanese students studying abroad dropped considerably. Students from Japan seemingly just wanted to stay home. In contrast, students studying abroad from Korea, China and India kept increasing. They were seeking more education and more international experience. Recently, Japanese students have started to study abroad again, but the numbers are still very low. 5

The reasons are not clear, but it seems that Japanese young people read about all the terrible things going on in the world, wars, mass shootings, bombings, and other horrors and decide to stay inside Japan. Are young people too frightened to leave the relative safety of Japan? It seems so, but why, I wonder. Maybe 10 they feel the world comes to them through the internet, but can the world really be experienced online? Maybe I am too old school in my thinking, but I firmly believe it is necessary to get out and be someplace different for a meaningful experience.

Of course, these days, Japanese students may be getting 15 more foreign culture and second language experiences inside Japan. The opportunities here to study English and have contact with people from other countries are numerous, especially in big cities. However, that is not the same as immersing oneself in another culture. Learning English without traveling abroad is like 20 buying a sports car and keeping it in your garage without driving it around.

Many students might worry that culture shock will be too great, but it is culture shock that helps people grow and develop. Becoming good at a foreign language and good at being interna- 25 tionalized depends on deep, and sometimes difficult, experiences. It is possible to consciously and deliberately learn English or other cultures without going abroad, but that is often a conscious act. It is the unconscious mind where culture shock appears. But that is also where deeper understanding develops. Studying abroad forces 30 an emotional depth of experience that is more than just information, grammar or basic knowledge.

Many students have a real inner struggle over this issue, and that is understandable. They want to see what lies outside the islands of Japan, but are worried about how difficult it is. All too often, that conflict is resolved by taking the easy route of just staying at home. Often that is because students lack confidence. All too often, schools, peers and families do not push students to take on smaller challenges as practice for taking on bigger challenges.

More foreigners are coming to visit Japan than ever before, so the future of the Japanese economy will increasingly depend on language skills and a global mindset. It is hard to conceive of many jobs that will not entail some international element in the future. Workplaces and lifestyles are influenced by trends from all around the world, and depend on them for their vital dynamic. Without experience abroad, Japanese will be at a disadvantage when dealing with foreigners who have more experience.

The challenge of studying abroad is one way to acquire valuable life skills and to develop one's mindset into one that adapts well to new and different situations. Dropping into a foreign culture and figuring out how to deal with other languages, foods, attitudes and ways of thinking forces young people not just to adapt, but to learn how to adapt.

For thousands of years, tribal cultures set up coming-of-age rituals for their young people. They taught them well as children, but at some point, they tested the young people by leaving them alone in the forest, or telling them to travel alone to a distant place, or doing some ritual activity that was dangerous. Those rituals helped them grow into adults by learning to rely on themselves. But in Japan, it is too easy to avoid that transition, and remain mired in a childhood mindset.

The education ministry is right to promote more students going abroad, not just to improve Japan's competitiveness in the world market, but to help students improve their own lives. My students who study abroad always come back with greater energy, 5 motivation and maturity. They also, ironically perhaps, always return loving Japan more than they did before.

Schools and parents should push young people to take up challenges, to become self-reliant and skilled in handling personal, educational and professional challenges. One way to do that is to 10 study abroad. The future of Japan will be shaped by the youthful experiences of Japanese young people. When I ask my students how their year abroad was, they invariably answer, "It was the best year of my life!"

I Using the keywords

In the blanks, put the most suitable word from the essay. More than one word might work, but choose the one that best fits.

1. Even if you feel _____ about giving your speech, you should go ahead and do it anyway.

2. The hardest but fastest way to learn a language is by _____ yourself in a situation where you cannot speak your mother tongue.

3. When you start to practice, you should do it very _____, but little by little it will become natural and you won't even think about it.

4. I thought this problem was already _____, but now you want to keep arguing about it?

5. One _____ to traveling when you are young is not having much money, but on the other hand you are open to experience and can learn a lot.

II Comprehending the essay

Review the essay and find the answers to these questions.

1. What are the possible reasons for Japanese young people not studying abroad?

   _____

2. According to the essay, is culture shock a bad thing?

   _____

3. How does studying abroad connect to the Japanese economy?

   _____

4. What does studying abroad teach about adapting?

   _____

5. Does studying abroad make young people dislike Japan?

   _____

6. What does the writer suggest at the end?

_____

Ⅲ Summarizing the essay

By reusing your answers to the comprehension questions, write a short summary of the essay in your own words.

_____
_____
_____
_____
_____
_____
_____
_____
_____
_____

Ⅳ Discussing ideas and opinions

Think about your opinion on each of these questions and discuss with other students in groups.

1. Do you think it is important to study abroad? Why or why not?

2. What are the main reasons young Japanese do not study abroad, in your opinion?

3. What will happen if Japanese workers do not have enough experience with foreign cultures and challenging situations?

Unit
15 Passion for English

🎧 DL 170 ~ 179　◉ CD2-72 ~ ◉ CD2-81

I met one of my former students for lunch at an Italian restaurant in Shinjuku, but I hardly got to say anything. She was leaving in a week to study art management at graduate school in England and was so excited about it, I could not get a word in
5　edgewise. Her enthusiasm bubbled over so much she barely ate any of the pizza. "Eat something," I'd say, and she'd take a bite before setting it back down and talking more. We, or rather, *she* talked for about two hours straight, all in fluent English!

She was not always so fluent and enthusiastic. When she
10　was in my seminar, she often missed class and performed below her level. When job-hunting season started, she disappeared more often before becoming totally burnt out. She finally took a job at a large company where she would never be able to use English. Even before graduating, she told me the introductory meetings at

the company were "boring." I got a card from her a couple years after she graduated, but heard nothing more.

Then, one day, I got an email asking if she could stop by my office. A week later, she came in, excited, and, before even sitting down announced, "I quit my job! I want to go study abroad!" 5 She stumbled and apologized, "I haven't spoken English in three years!" Her job, she explained, was just not right for her. She wanted to use English to study something related to art, but was not quite sure how to do that. However, as if it was a lecture class, she took out a pen and started taking notes on what I said, nod- 10 ding her head and smiling, happy to hear English again and to have changed her life direction.

From there, she started conversation lessons and signed up for an intensive test prep class. She dipped into her savings to pay for an English school in New York for six weeks, and then traveled 15 all over America to look at schools. She came back to Tokyo and took another English test prep class. Little by little, she narrowed down her interests to art management, a field that combined her passion for English and her passion for art, and yet still had a practical focus that could lead to a job in the future. Each time she 20 emailed me, her English was a little better than before. Finally, this email arrived: "Sensei, I've been accepted in art management at a British university! I'm leaving in a week. Can you meet me for lunch before I go?"

Her passion for English waxed and waned through her life. 25 She loved English when very young, then hated it during the entrance exam period, loved it again during the last two years of college, and gave it up altogether after graduating. Then her passion came back and helped shift her direction in life. Most students, unfortunately, give up their passion for English and never get it 30 back.

This passion for English is something that burns in many students, but often the flame is too weak. A couple bad teachers, a boring class or two, or even a bad grade on an essay can cause students to lose their passion for English. And that is just for the students who survive the anesthetization of entrance exams. Studying English is a multi-year marathon in which students can give up anywhere along the way and never get back in the race.

The most common story is that students love studying English when the basics are easy, but then get lost at advanced levels. Often, they have not acquired the skills or habits, other than test taking, to keep studying at advanced levels where studying depends on one's own motivation. At higher levels, the one subject some students really love becomes a recipe for frustration. Instead of working for success, many students end up with a sense of failure that affects their entire life.

Sometimes, too, students become too narrowly focused on English, without developing other interests, like art or music or business. At a certain level, English study starts to gradually expand into related interests. Most people who study English begin to use it for work, travel, relationships, other subjects, or personal interests. That is, their passion for English spreads out into other passions. Pushing them away from their passions is the call of comfort and an easy life. Other students are too narrowly focused—just on English itself. If they do not use English for other purposes, their studies stop. Many students' passion for English takes them to where they can see an interesting new direction in their lives. But if they do not have passion, they cannot take themselves in that new direction.

Of course, everyone must give up some youthful pursuits as

they get older and passion cools. The realities of life sink in. However, seeing the loss of passion too young is one of the most disappointing aspects of my job. When students who really love English give up on it too easily or too soon, I feel frustrated and dismayed.

The writer Stephen Leacock said, "It may be those who do 5 most, dream most." Dreaming, which is the story form of passion, is what keeps people going to do more things in life. Passion generates more passion, and for the difficult, tiring, long-term study of English, passion is essential.

I Using the keywords

In the blanks, put the most suitable word from the essay. More than one word might work, but choose the one that best fits.

1. That is my _____ boyfriend, but we broke up a long time ago.
2. Because the class was so difficult, no one had any _____ for the exam. They gave up studying.
3. I tried to explain myself, but I _____ over my words and could not say what I wanted to.
4. For every difficult thing you try, you will always encounter some _____. The important thing is to keep going anyway.
5. I was very _____ that none of my group members showed up and I had to do the presentation myself.

II Comprehending the essay

Review the essay and find the answers to these questions.

1. What happened with the writer's student?

   _____

2. What did the student do to get ready to study abroad?

   _____

3. Did the student always love English?

   _____

4. Why do some students lose their passion for English?

   _____

5. Is passion important for studying, according to this essay?

   _____

Ⅲ Summarizing the essay

By reusing your answers to the comprehension questions, write a short summary of the essay in your own words.

_____

_____

_____

_____

_____

_____

_____

_____

_____

_____

Ⅳ Discussing ideas and opinions

Think about your opinion on each of these questions and discuss with other students in groups.

1. Can the education system sometimes kill students' passion? Why is that?
2. Why do many students give up on studying English?
3. What is your deepest passion except for English? Do you have a passion for English?

NOTES

Unit 1　What's in a Name?

Title　**What's in a Name?**「名前が何だっていうんだ？」ウィリアム・シェイクスピア（1564-1616）の *Romeo and Juliet*（『ロミオとジュリエット』）の第2幕第2場の Juliet のセリフから。「名前の中に何がある？（何もないではないか）」という反語表現になっており、「重要なのは中身である」という意味を表す慣用表現として用いられる。

10　7　*Moby Dick*「『白鯨』」1851年に出版されたハーマン・メルヴィルの小説。捕鯨船の船長エイハブが巨大な白いマッコウクジラの Moby Dick に復讐を挑む物語で、世界の十大小説のひとつと称される。

　　　Herman Melville「ハーマン・メルヴィル（1819-1891）」アメリカの小説家。難解な作風で知られる。

　　8　**"Call me Ishmael."**「私のことはイシュメイルと呼んでくれ」『白鯨』の有名な冒頭の一節。Ishmael は『白鯨』の語り手であり、主人公である Ahab とともに旧約聖書の人物から名を取られている。

　　9　**self-definition**「自己定義、自己認識」

　　　peg「（服や帽子などを掛ける）フック」

　　10　**not that simple**「それほど単純ではない」

　　11　**a term of respect**「敬語」

　　12　**hierarchy**「階層、ヒエラルキー」ピラミッド形の上下関係を持つ組織や秩序。

　　13　**duties to dispense**「分配すべき課題」

11　5　**terms of address**「呼びかけ方」

　　6　**devolves into ...**「堕落して（退化して）…になる」

　　6-　**a puzzling jumble of inconsistencies with foreign names**「人を当惑させる、外国人の名前の相互に矛盾した呼び方のごたまぜ」

　　7　**On any given day**「来る日も来る日も」

　　16　**frequent**「…（特定の場所）をよく訪れる」

　　20　**city office**「市役所」

　　28　**go together**「両立する」

12　1　**protocol**「プロトコル」国際的な交際における正式な礼儀作法。外交儀礼。

　　4　**awkward**「気まずい」

　　4-　**leave it as it is**「それを今のままにしておく」

　　6　**When speaking English**「英語を話す際」When の後に they are が省略されている。

　　6-　**refer to other colleagues by their first name**「他の同僚をファーストネームで呼ぶ」

　　11　**As with ...**「…と同様に」

　　13　**application forms**「申込用紙」

14	**adapt and bend my name**「私の名前を変化させて曲げる」ここでは記入欄に合わせて名前を改変、つまり歪曲するということ。
26	**rotating**「交替する」
27	**tangled**「混乱した、こんがらがった」
29	**joint venture**「合弁事業」
13　3	**spouses**「配偶者」
9	**consistency**「一貫性」
11	**avatar**「アバター、化身」

Unit 2　Country of Eyes

page　line

16　2	**the contest of "who will look away first."**「『どちらが先に目をそらすか』の競争」
4	**outstared**「…をより長く見つめた」
	humiliated「自尊心が傷つけられた」
7	**bewildered**「戸惑っている」
8	**alienated**「疎外されている」
11	**humility**「謙遜、謙虚さ」
	clamp down「ギュッと閉じる」ここでは「目を合わせてもらえない」という意味。
17　4	**linger**「とどまる、後に残る」
5	**cut in front of ...**「…の前に割り込む」
7-	**masters of the side-glance and the stolen glance**「横目で見たり、見ないふりをして見たり（盗み見したり）する達人」
13	**crept into ...**「（知らないうちに）…に入り込んだ」
14	**holler out**「大声を出して伝える、はっきりとものを言う」
14-	**"Hey, how ya doin'?"**「やあ、元気？」how are you doing? のくだけた言い方。
18-	**Keeping one's eyes cast downward**「視線を落としたままにすること」
22	**startled**「驚いた」
28-	**safe inside the technological insulation of their cellphone and earphones**「携帯電話やイヤホンといった科学技術によって保護されており安全である」insulation「隔離、保護」
30	**passing image**「通り過ぎていく人影」
18　1	**Johnny Depp**「ジョニー・デップ（1963-)」『パイレーツ・オブ・カリビアン』シリーズや『チャーリーとチョコレート工場』などで知られるアメリカの俳優。
8	**retreating deeper inside themselves**「自分自身の殻により深く引きこもる」retreat「後退する」
11	**civility**「礼儀正しさ、礼節」
15-	**a circuit is connected**「（意思疎通の）回路がつながる」双方向の意思疎通の土壌が形成されていることを示す。
21	**ocular intimacy**「視覚を通じて親交を結ぶこと」ocular「目の」
28	**perusing**「…をじっくり見ること」

29 **unfathomable**「測りがたい、深遠な」

29- **What could be more beautiful and mysterious than human eyes?**「人の視線よりも美しく謎めいたものなどありうるだろうか」仮定法の could を用いた反語表現で、ありえないという断定の意を強めている。次の What could be more human? も同様。

19　5 **brief as it is**「短時間だけれども」形容詞 + as + S（主語）+ be 動詞で「S は…だけれども」の意味を表す。

Unit 3　The Language Dance

22　2 **the dance of a honeybee**「ミツバチのダンス」ミツバチは餌となる花の蜜の場所を仲間に伝える際、「8 の字ダンス」と呼ばれる動きでコミュニケーションを行う。

　　5 **what language to engage in**「何語を使うか」

　　7 **it occasionally turns out**「折に触れてわかることだが」

　　9 **ritual**「儀式的な」ここでは形容詞として用いられているが、次の行では「儀式」という意味の名詞として用いられている。

　　13 **kind of test the waters**「それとなく様子をうかがう」test the waters は「ちょっとずつ水をかける」が転じて「様子をうかがう」という意味を表す。

　　14 **Presto**「直ちに」音楽の速度記号として「急速に」という意味をもつイタリア語で、ここでは直ちに英語での会話に切り替わることを表している。マジシャンが用いるかけ声で「ほら（うまくいった）、あら不思議」という意味もある。

23　2 **non-presto**「直ちにではなく」直ちに英語での会話に切り替わるのではなく、言葉のダンスが続く様子を表している。

　　3 **take several polite rounds**「数回ていねいなやりとりをする」
settle on ...「…を決める」

　　4- **depending on our relative language levels, relative pride, or relative fatigue**「おたがいの言語レベル、プライドの高さ、もしくは疲労の程度によって」

　　7 **grappling for the strongest hold**「最も力が入る組み手を求めて組み合っている」

　　9- **stammering drunk about ...**「…について酔って言葉をつかえながら話しかけてくる」この drunk は「酔っぱらった状態で」という意味の副詞で、stammering を修飾している。

　　11 **random strangers**「行き当たりばったりの見知らぬ人たち」

　　17 **double strangers**「二重の意味での他人」見知らぬ人であり外国人であるという意味。

　　19 **is gaining hold**「力を増しつつある」

　　22 **craft beer**「クラフトビール」小規模な醸造所で伝統的な製法で作られるビール。

　　24 **a pint**「1 杯のビール」1 パイント = 0.473 リットル。
stole furtive glances at ...「…を盗み見た」furtive glance「盗み見」

　　25 *sotto voce*「小声で、ささやくように」音楽用語で、*sotto* は「下に」、voce は「声」

という意味のイタリア語。次の *sotto*（そっと）にかけた言葉遊びになっている。

29 **obligated**「義務付けられた」

30 ***my* language**「私の言語」イタリック体は強調のため強く発音されることを示す。同じ行の *hers* も同様。

24 1 **lean over for ...**「…に気持ちが傾く」
   Fair enough.「わかった、結構だ」

4 **in which case**「そして、その場合」

4- **my forcing them into English**「私が彼らに英語を強制すること」forcing は動名詞で、my は forcing の意味上の主語。

7 **in case ...**「…するといけないので、…する場合に備えて」

8 **is not up to it**「それに耐えられない」be up to ... はここでは「…に耐える、…の能力がある」の意味。

9 **figuring out ...**「…を見極めながら、…を見つけ出しながら」

11 **All of that happens in a few conversational turns**「そういったすべてのことが、数回にわたる会話のやりとりの中で起こる」

15 **loosen up**「打ち解けて話す」

16 **mindsets**「ものの見方、考え方」

25 4 **peek over at ...**「…を覗き見る」

5 **prepping for ...**「…の準備をしている、…に備えている」

6- **the bedraggled student**「（勉強に集中するあまり）髪や服が整っていないその生徒」

8- **as if magically conjured from the pages of the book**「まるで本のページから魔法で呼び起こされたかのように」conjure「（魔法で）…を呼び出す」

16 **still unsure how to pull the words off the page and let them live**「ページから言葉を引っ張り出し、それらに命を吹き込む方法がいまだにわからないけれど」

Unit 4　Japan Open and Closed

page　line

28 3 **picky about ...**「…の好みがうるさい」

29 3 **receptivity**「受容力、受容性」cf. receptive「受け入れようとする、受容的な」

7 **a huge reserve of ...**「たくさん蓄えられた…」

8 **unquestioned**「疑問視されない、絶対的な」

9- **onslaught of ...**「圧倒されるほど膨大な…」

14 **exasperating**「腹立たしい」

18 **be in a standoff with ...**「…と膠着状態にある、…とにらみ合いの状態にある」

19 **Japan is as much an idea as a location**「日本とは場所であると同時に概念でもある」as much A as B「B と同じくらいに A、B するだけの量の A」

20 **divided against itself**「内輪もめしている」ここでは「意見が分かれて分裂している」という意味。

21 **conformist**「（体制・習慣などに）順応的な」

22	**poised for ...**「…に備えて」
	initial charge「（相撲の）立ち合い」
23	**out-of-the-way**「人通りを離れた」
25	**a hunkering looking-away**「前かがみになって目をそらす」hunker「背を曲げる、前かがみになる」
30	**If anything**「それどころか」
30　1	**messing up ...**「…を台無しにすること」
3-	**appetizer**「前菜」
16	**born of ...**「…から生まれる、…から生じる」
31　2	**pulled into ...**「（車が）…に入った」
3	**the disorganized taxi line**「バラバラにタクシーを待つ客の列」
5-	**one that would have been impossible in years past**「何年も前だったらありえなかったようなもの」仮定法過去完了の構文。one は代名詞で直前の compliment を指す。
11	**iron grip**「強い支配力」
13	**odd fads**「おかしな流行」
16	**The sheer range of ...**「広範囲に及ぶ…」
19	**By which I mean**「つまり」

Unit 5　Why Ask Me?

page　line

34　4-	**a few more ramen specialty questions**「さらに2、3のラーメンに関する専門的な質問」
5-	**other ingredients**「他の材料」ここではコショウや酢、ニンニクなどを指す。
7	**slurping**「スープをすすること」
8	**interrogation**「尋問」
14-	**with "Can you use chopsticks?" being the classic**「『あなたはお箸は使えますか？』という質問は代表的なものだ」with + O（目的語）+ 現在分詞で「O が…している状態で」という意味。
35　1-	**the cultural dividing line**「文化を分け隔てるライン」
4	**a bit of heaven**「ちょっとした天国」
7	**I do draw a line at *shiokara*.**「私は塩辛には絶対手を出さない」draw a line at ...「…に手を出さない、…まではやらない」
15-	**no one would ask a foreign visitor if they enjoy eating a juicy steak**「誰も外国人訪問者に彼らがジューシーなステーキを食べて楽しんでいるかどうか尋ねないだろう」この would は仮定法過去の用法。
17	**a given**「当たり前のもの」
24	**savoring**「…を楽しんでいる」savor「…を味わう、…を楽しむ」
25	**individual enlightenment**「個人的な悟り」
30	**an automatic copyright to ...**「…に対して自動的に著作権を持つこと」
36　2-	**apprentice yourself for years to a master pottery craftsman**「何年間も

陶磁器職人の親方の弟子になる」apprentice oneself to ...「…の弟子になる」

	9	**justifiable pride**「もっともと思えるプライド」
	12	**broader considerations**「より広範囲にわたる考察」
	14	**cultural imperative**「文化的命令、文化的要請」
	15	**a way of re-claiming heritage**「文化遺産を返還要求するひとつの方法」
37	5	**tap into ...**「…を引き出す」
	19	**hidden-away**「見えないところに隠れている」
	21	**acclaim**「拍手喝采」= acclamation
	22-	**As for ramen, how much more universally lovable a lunch could there be?**「ラーメンに関して言えば、より普遍的に愛されるランチが他にありうるだろうか？」仮定法を用いた反語表現で、ラーメン以上に愛されるランチはないということを言っている。

Unit 6 Politics So Far from Home

page line

40	3	**classic rock radio**「ロックの名曲専門のラジオ局」
	6	**pull**「魅力」
	7	**brashness**「厚かましさ」
		posturing「ジェスチャー、ポーズ、見せかけの行動、駆け引き」
	7-	**outspokenness**「率直さ、歯に衣着せぬ物言い」
	8	**perch**「止まり木」安全な場所のたとえ。
	10	**in this day and age**「今日では」
	12	**gaffe**「失言」
	12-	**pronouncement**「声明」
41	3	**overt**「あからさまな」
	4	**hilarious**「抱腹絶倒の」
	5	**sarcastic**「皮肉な、辛らつな」
	6	**moron**「まぬけ」
		"True that!"「『その通り！』」
	9	**on a daily basis**「日常的に、毎日」
	10	**proclaim**「…を公表する、…を明らかにする」
		politics「政治的意見」
	15	**as it usually happens**「通常起こることだが」
	18	**LDP**「自由民主党」Liberal Democratic Party の略。
	19	**Communist**「日本共産党」正式には Japanese Communist Party という。
		squirm「（恥ずかしくて）もじもじする」
42	1	**as do most of my colleagues**「私の大半の同僚がそうするように」この do は squirm and frown の代動詞であり、主語 most of my colleagues と倒置の関係にある。
	3	**ignite**「…（論争など）を引き起こす発端となる、…に火をつける」
	6	**election primaries**「予備選挙」アメリカ大統領選挙において各政党が候補者

を指名するための選挙。

7 **relish**「…に喜びを感じる」

8 **"Let's agree to disagree,"**「『意見の違いということにしておこう』」意見がまとまらないときなどに用いられる決まり文句。

12 **through unspoken means**「言葉に出すのとは別の方法で」

16 **absentee ballot**「不在者投票」

17 **small-minded**「狭量な」
out-of-touch「現実を知らない、情報に疎い」

21 **default**「デフォルト、（コンピューターの）初期設定」

22 **aggravated**「いらいらしている、怒っている」

23 **Republicans**「（アメリカの）共和党員」
Democrats「（アメリカの）民主党員」

25 **enrage**「…を激怒させる」

28 **chronic**「常習的な」

28- **instinctive**「本能的な」

43 1 **spout**「…（意見・自説など）をベラベラとまくしたてる、…をとうとうと述べる」

5 **What you feel is where you live.**「あなたが心に感じている国こそが、あなたが本当に住んでいる国である」あなたの気持ちが向く国が、あなたが本当に住んでいる国であるという意味。

8 **representatives**「議員」ここではアメリカの下院議員を指す。

12- **prominently**「目立つように」

Unit 7 Is Japan in Decline?

page line

46 1 **in decline**「衰退の道をたどっている」

2 **disheartening**「がっかりさせるような」

3 **stalled economy**「失速した経済」
stagnant「停滞気味の」

4 **the weight of providing for a graying population**「高齢化している人々を扶養するという重荷」provide for ...「…を養う」

5 **out of touch with ...**「…とかけ離れている、…に疎い」

8 **economic analysts**「経済評論家」

9 **in the short term**「短期的に」

10- **does not inspire optimism**「楽観的見方を呼び起こさない」

12- **profit-oriented criteria**「営利・利益志向の基準」-oriented「…志向の」。criteria は criterion の複数形。

47 1 **economics-based**「経済状態をふまえた」

2 **"bubble era,"**「『バブルの時代』」1986年末から1991年初めにかけて、日本では株価や地価などの資産価格が急激に上昇して空前の好景気に沸いた。その発生と崩壊を bubble（泡）に例えてこのように呼ぶ。
booming「好景気の、成長著しい」

current picture「現在の情勢、現状」
4 overpraised「過度に賞賛された」
6 business practices「商習慣、ビジネス手法」
11- "Japan-bashers."「『日本叩きをする人たち』」
13 socialistic「社会主義的な」
15 short-sightedness「先見の明のなさ」
enduringly「永続的に」
16 exam-obsessed「試験のことで頭がいっぱいの」
18- a grinding place of overtime and exhaustion and unfairness「残業、過労、そして不平等だらけの過酷な場所」
22 took too extreme a view「あまりにも極端な考え方、見方をしていた」a（n）＋形容詞＋名詞に too を用いると、一般的には too ＋形容詞＋ a（n）＋名詞の語順になり、「あまりにも…な〜」という意味を表す。
30 skyscrapers scrape the sky「超高層ビルが空にそびえている」scrape「…をこする」
48 2 be redoing ...「…を作り変えている、…を改装している」
4 economic figures「経済的な数字、経済統計」
6 sluggishness「不況」
10 retail companies「小売企業」
15 overtake「…に追いつく、…を追い抜く」
49 5 overhaul「全面的な見直し」
oppressive「抑圧的な、息詰まるような」
5- Without addressing these problems「これらの問題に取り組まなければ」
6 tip to ...「…に傾く」
8 a positive「肯定的な側面」
balance ... out「…の帳尻を合わせる」
9 social cohesion「社会の団結、一体性」
10 group mentality「集団主義」
20 in equal measures「同等に、同程度に」

Unit 8　A New Era or An Era of Newness?

page line
52 2- not so much the name itself, Reiwa, as how it was chosen「令和という名称そのものよりもむしろその選ばれ方」not so much A as B「A というよりもむしろ B」
4- cabinet members「閣僚」
5 bureaucratic committees「官僚からなる委員会」
6- the Imperial Household Agency「宮内庁」
9- got off on the wrong foot「出だしで失敗した」
10 rankled「…を苦しめた」
13 restricted「一般には非公開の」

14 **sacred grounds**「神聖な場所」

53 2 **chrysanthemum images**「菊の御紋」
rice stalks「稲穂」

2- **intensely colored silk costumes**「強い色調の絹の衣装」

7- **It was as if Japan had a new mental and spiritual OS installed.**「まるで日本は新しい精神的、霊的 OS をインストールされたみたいだった」have + O（目的語）＋過去分詞で「O を…される、O を…してもらう」という意味を表す。OS とは operating system の略で、コンピューターを動かす基本ソフトウェアのこと。

11 **what the future will hold**「どんな将来が待ち受けているか」

14 **rejuvenation**「再生」
revitalization「再活性」

18 **taking up challenges**「難題に立ち向かう、挑戦に応じる」

19 **introverted**「内向的な、引っ込み思案な」

24 **holding ... back**「…を食い止める、…を引き止める」

27 **feel stifled**「息苦しさを感じる」

28 **skill sets**「（持っている）知能や技能」

54 1 **underrepresented**「少数しか存在しない」
positions of power「権力のある地位」

1- **getting around ...**「…を克服する」

8 **vibrancy**「活気」

13 **OECD**「経済協力開発機構」主に欧米の先進国が中心となり、経済発展に尽力する国際機関。Organization for Economic Cooperation and Development の略。

26- **allotted vacation time**「有給休暇」allotted「割り当てられた」

29 **time off**「（学校・仕事の）休み」

55 6 **spur a deeper look at ...**「…についてさらに深く見るよう刺激する」spur「…を促す」

9 **initiative**「先導力」

9- **momentum**「勢い」

Unit 9 Earthquake Life

page line

58 2 **about to be pounced on**「今にも襲いかかられそうな」about to ...「まさに…しようとしている」、pounce on ...「…に飛びかかる」
predator「捕食者、肉食動物」

2- **adrenaline pumping**「アドレナリンがどっと出て」adrenaline が pumping の主語となる独立分詞構文。

4 **Often as they come**「（地震は）しょっちゅう起こるけれど」副詞＋ as ＋ S（主語）＋ V（動詞）で「S は…だけれども」という意味を表す。

8 **sublet apartment**「また借りのアパート」

10- **I am from Kansas, home of tornados.**「私は竜巻のメッカであるカンザスの

出身だ」アメリカの児童文学作家ライマン・フランク・ボームの *The Wizard of Oz*（『オズの魔法使い』）はカンザスを舞台としており、主人公の少女ドロシーと飼い犬のトトは家ごと竜巻に巻き込まれてオズの国へと飛ばされる。

12 **It made a great letter home.**「故郷に大きな知らせとなった」

13 **unpredictability**「予測が不可能であること」

59 11- **out-plan, out-think, out-prepare them**「それら（地震）に対してしっかり計画し、しっかり考え、しっかり備える」接頭辞の out- は動詞に付いて「…を上回る、…を凌駕する」の意味を付与する。

16 **when it comes to ...**「…に関しては、…のことになると」

17 **clam up**「黙り込む」

19 **that stoic attitude**「あの冷静な態度」

20 **approach to ...**「…のやり方」この to は前置詞のため目的語は動名詞（ignoring）となる。

22 **It works pretty well.**「それで結構うまくいくのだ」

23- **It seems a baffling mix of passive acceptance, pragmatic realism and transcendence.**「それは、ありのままを受け入れる姿勢と、実際的な現実主義と、そして超越的な姿勢が混じり合っているようで、（筆者にとっては）まごつくばかりである」

26 **kind of get it**「なんとなく理解できる」

60 8- **unobtrusive**「（態度などが）控えめな、出しゃばらない」

10 **A newly aware mindset**「新たに意識するようになったものの見方」

11 **fatalities**「犠牲者たち」

14 **became a little less of a stranger**「それほど他人でもなくなった」

15 **discombobulated**「困惑した」アメリカの俗語。

18 **let out of ...**「…から追い出された」

18- **I went through the motions of ...**「…のあらゆる行為を一通りやった」

22 **stuck to ...**「…に固執した、…をし続けた」

29 **branded them *"fly-jin,"***「『フライジン』という呼び名をつけた」brand「…に烙印を押す、…に汚名を着せる」
rhyme「韻を踏んだ言葉」

30 **deprecating word**「軽蔑的な言葉」
edgy「神経が高ぶった」

61 1- **nerve-rattling aftershocks**「神経を参らせるような余震」

12 **rekindle**「…をよみがえらせる、…をもう一度呼び覚ます」

12- **the hopeful energy that I always felt was the engine of Japanese life**「いつも私が日本人の生活の原動力だと感じていた希望に満ちた活力」that [I always felt] was ... として関係代名詞＋挿入節と考える。

Unit 10　Integrating Immigrants

page　line

64 7- **They could not have been nicer, even though I was probably the first**

foreigner ever to have a bank account there.「私がおそらくそこで銀行口座を持とうとした初めての外国人であったにもかかわらず、彼らはそれ以上はないほど親切だった」仮定法過去完了を用いた比較級の文だが意味としては最上級を表している。

65　1　**back then**「その当時」

　　2　**strike up ...**「…を始める」

　　9　**an authentic experience of Japan**「日本の本物の経験」

　　11　**stand-offish**「打ち解けない」

　　16　**insular communities**「閉鎖的なコミュニティ」insular「島のように孤立した」

　　20-　**the Ghibli Museum**「三鷹の森ジブリ美術館」東京都三鷹市にあるアニメーションの美術館。スタジオジブリ関連の展示品を多く収蔵・公開している。

66　2　**mixed heritage**「混成した文化的背景」たとえば両親の国籍が異なると、その子どもは混成した文化的背景を持つことになる。

　　7　**resilience**「回復力」

　　10　**cuisine**「料理（法）、調理（法）」

　　16　**cohesiveness**「結束力」

　　17-　**a gentle wearing away of ...**「…を徐々に弱めること」

　　18　**inflexible**「柔軟性のない、融通の利かない」

　　24　**A deeper integration of immigrants**「海外からの移住者たちとのより深いレベルでの共生」

　　27　**Cultures in proximity**「近接した状態にあるさまざまな文化」proximity「近いこと」

67　2　**heterogeneous**「異種（混成）の」

　　4-　**an already vibrant homogenous culture**「既存の活気に満ちた同質の文化」homogenous「同質の」

　　6　**blips and glitches**「音声の途切れと計器の不調」日本への移住者が増えるにつれて、いろんな摩擦が起こるであろうということの比喩表現。

　　8-　**an interactive, synergistic blend**「相互的で、相乗効果を生む混合」

　　10　**dwell on ...**「…についてあれこれ考える」

Unit 11　The Right Amount of Confidence

page　line

72　3　**And they mean it!**「そして彼らは本気でそう言っているのだ！」

　　6　**Hipsters**「流行の先端を行く人」

　　8　**self-pity**「自己憐憫」

　　12　**teeth-sucking**「舌打ちする」

73　4　**Bragging**「自慢すること」

　　6　**unassuming**「偉そうにしない、（能力などを）ひけらかさない」

　　8　**put on an act of ...**「…のふりをする」
　　　self-possession「落着き、冷静沈着」
　　　grating「（行動などが）いらだたせる、不快にさせる」

Unit 12 Mistake Makers of the World, Unite!

79	1	**a single unifying characteristic**「唯一の統一的な特徴」
	6	**look through ...**「…を調べる」
	11	**hand back ...**「…を手渡しで返す」
	12	**make students redo the form of their work**「学生に作文の形式面の書き直しをさせる」
	17-	**just listen to kids in their first language**「子どもたちが初めて発する言葉に少し耳を傾けてみればよい」
	19	**go through ...**「…を経験する」
		language growth spurt「語学力が急成長すること」
	22	**rambling on**「とりとめなく話し続ける」
	23	**a bunch of ...**「たくさんの…」
	25	**stony-faced**「無表情の」
	30-	**shell-shocked survivors of chronic correction**「長期にわたって間違いを正され、大きなショックを受けながらも耐え抜いてきた者」shell-shocked「大きなショックを受けて」
80	4	**a constant flow of language**「ひとつの流れのように絶え間なく言葉を発すること」
	7	**no big deal**「大したことはない」
	12-	**at the very best**「せいぜい」
	18-	**"words, words, words,"**「『言葉、言葉、言葉』」ウィリアム・シェイクスピアの悲劇 *Hamlet*（『ハムレット』）第2幕第2場における主人公ハムレットの台詞。
	19-	**good laugh**「大笑い」
81	3	**ingrained**「心に植え付けられた」

Unit 13 The Art of Conversation

page	line	
84	6	**art, not structure**「（会話の）技術であって、文の構造ではない」
	12	**personal warmth**「人間としての温かみ」
85	1-	**condensable into worksheets and right and wrong answers for tests**「練習問題用紙とテストの問題の正解・不正解に凝縮できる」
	2-	**a definite starting and stopping point**「明確な出発点と終着点」
	4	**messy**「面倒な、厄介な」
		undefined「はっきりしない」
	5	**get going**「始める」
86	4	**so-so**「まあまあの、よくも悪くもない」
	9	**rests on ...**「…に基づく」
	11	**conversationalists**「話し上手」
	20	**conversation starters**「会話を切り出す話題」
	21	**follow-up questions**「補足質問」
		open style questions「Yes か No で答えられない質問」
	23	**non-verbal 'tricks'**「言葉をつかわない『芸当』」

Unit 14 "Get Out! Why Not Go?"

Unit 15 Passion for English

することができる、…する機会を得る」

3　**art management**「アートマネジメント、芸術経営学」芸術・文化活動を支援して社会に普及させる方法論や仕組み。
　　graduate school「大学院」

4-　**get a word in edgewise**「口を挟む」

5　**bubbled over**「沸き立った、あふれんばかりだった」

6-　**"Eat something," I'd say, and she'd take a bite before setting it back down and talking more.**「『何か食べたら』と私が言うと、彼女はひと口食べてはそれを戻してさらにしゃべった」I'd と she'd は I would と she would の省略形。would を繰り返して、「…してはまた…した」という交互に反復された行動を意味する。take a bite「ひと口食べる」

8　**straight**「途切れることなく」

12　**burnt out**「燃え尽きて、疲れ果てて」

14　**introductory meetings**「初顔合わせの会合」

97　2　**heard nothing more**「それっきり音沙汰がなかった」

3　**stop by ...**「…に立ち寄る」

13-　**signed up for ...**「…に申し込む、…に登録する」

14　**an intensive test prep class**「テスト準備集中コース」
　　dipped into her savings「自分の貯金を惜しみなく使った」dip into「(貯金に)手をつける」

17-　**narrowed down ...**「…の範囲を限定した、…を絞った」

19-　**a practical focus**「現実的な焦点」

25　**waxed and waned**「高まっては衰えた」

98　6　**the anesthetization of entrance exams**「入学試験による麻痺状態」受験勉強で英語が嫌いになる状態のことを言っている。anesthetization「麻酔状態、麻痺状態」

14　**a recipe for frustration**「挫折感のもと」

15-　**a sense of failure**「挫折感、敗北感」

23-　**the call of comfort and an easy life**「快適さと楽な人生の誘惑」

99　1　**sink in**「身に染みる」

4　**give up on ...**「…に見切りをつける、…を断念する」

5　**Stephen Leacock**「スティーブン・リーコック (1869-1944)」イギリスで生まれ、両親とカナダに渡り、後にマギル大学教授となった。ユーモアと風刺あふれる作家としても知られ、代表作には *Sunshine Sketches of a Little Town*（『小さな町の陽気なスケッチ』）がある。カナダでは、毎年出版される最もユーモアのある作品に対して、彼の名を冠したスティーブン・リーコック・ユーモア賞が与えられている。

5-　**"It may be those who do most, dream most."**「『最も多くをなす人は、最も多く夢見る人であろう』」

本書には音声CD（別売）があります

Inbound/Outbound Japan
その先の日本へ──新しい日本の私たち

2020年1月20日　初版第1刷発行
2022年9月10日　初版第5刷発行

著　者　Michael Pronko
編注者　玉　井　久　之
　　　　安　田　　優
　　　　田　代　直　也
　　　　橋　本　史　帆
　　　　橋　野　朋　子

発行者　福　岡　正　人
発行所　株式会社　金星堂
（〒101-0051）東京都千代田区神田神保町 3-21
Tel. (03) 3263-3828（営業部）
　　（03) 3263-3997（編集部）
Fax (03) 3263-0716
http://www.kinsei-do.co.jp

編集担当　今門貴浩　　　　　　　Printed in Japan
印刷所／日新印刷株式会社　製本所／松島製本

ISBN978-4-7647-4102-7　C1082